EASY
MEALS *with*
BUILT-IN
PORTION
CONTROL!

the muffin tin cookbook

200 Fast, Delicious Mini-Pies, Pasta Cups, Gourmet Pockets, Veggie Cakes, and More!

Brette Sember
with Melinda Boyd, MPH, MHR, RD

Aadamsmedia
Avon, Massachusetts

Published by
Adams Media, a division of F+W Media, Inc.
57 Littlefield Street, Avon, MA 02322. U.S.A.
www.adamsmedia.com

ISBN 10: 1-4405-3216-8
ISBN 13: 978-1-4405-3216-0
eISBN 10: 1-4405-3618-X
eISBN 13: 978-1-4405-3618-2

Printed in the United States of America.

10   9   8   7   6   5   4   3   2   1

Library of Congress Cataloging-in-Publication Data
is available from the publisher.

Readers are urged to take all appropriate precautions before undertaking any how-to task. Always read and follow instructions and safety warnings for all tools and materials, and call in a professional if the task stretches your abilities too far. Although every effort has been made to provide the best possible information in this book, neither the publisher nor the author are responsible for accidents, injuries, or damage incurred as a result of tasks undertaken by readers. This book is not a substitute for professional services.

This publication is designed to provide accurate and authoritative information with regard to the subject matter covered. It is sold with the understanding that the publisher is not engaged in rendering legal, accounting, or other professional advice. If legal advice or other expert assistance is required, the services of a competent professional person should be sought.
—From a *Declaration of Principles* jointly adopted by a Committee of the American Bar Association and a Committee of Publishers and Associations

Many of the designations used by manufacturers and sellers to distinguish their product are claimed as trademarks. Where those designations appear in this book and Adams Media was aware of a trademark claim, the designations have been printed with initial capital letters.

This book is available at quantity discounts for bulk purchases.
For information, please call 1-800-289-0963.

contents

Chapter 9
Desserts 193

introduction

muffin tin cooking is fun, exciting, and creative! With your muffin tins you can create just about every type of dish imaginable (entrées, vegetables, potatoes, desserts, appetizers, and more).

Muffin tin dishes are easy to serve, easy to pass, and easy to share at a party or at your family table, or to savor just by yourself. Children especially enjoy being served muffin tin food. Muffin tin foods are also easy to store. Just pop the individual cups into a storage container, or simply cover your muffin tin with plastic wrap or foil. Cleanup is easy, too. If you use paper or foil liners, you throw them out or recycle them.

The best part is that these dishes are portion controlled. You know exactly how big a serving actually is, and there's no fooling yourself that you'll just have a tiny bit more of something. If you want more, you have to help yourself to another cup. One muffin cup is one serving, and that's that.

Muffin Tin Types

Today there are more choices than ever when it comes to muffin tins. Regular muffin tins (without nonstick coating) do still exist but may take some work to find. You may even find cast iron muffin tins, stoneware tins, or ceramic tins. Ceramic and stoneware tins are nice if you like to serve directly from the tin itself, because they are decorative. Nonstick muffin tins are popular because the nonstick coating keeps your dishes from sticking. Don't put all your faith in nonstick coating, though! Always spray a nonstick muffin tin with cooking spray before using. It is also a very good idea to spray the top of the muffin tin (the flat spaces in between the cups), because you may drop food there while filling the cups and the spray will help you clean it up.

Always read the care instructions that come with your tins and follow them. Dry your tins completely to avoid any problems with rust. Also be sure when you are baking with your tins that any empty cups in the tin are completely clean (if not, you will just bake on whatever is there).

Disposable aluminum muffin tins are handy if you're taking food somewhere but don't have a dependable carrier to put your cups in. Just bake them in the disposable tins (spray the tins with cooking spray first, or use liners), and they are easy to transport.

Silicone muffin tins are a recent addition to the market. These pans are soft and flexible and bake in a metal holder, or can stand on a baking sheet. They make it easy to push food out of the muffin cups without sticking, but their flexibility can mean your food might come out in pieces, as the flexibility can be difficult to control. Specialty silicone muffin pans now come in specific shapes, such as dinosaurs or stars, which are fun for children's parties or holidays.

Muffin Tin Sizes

Muffin pans themselves come in many sizes. Regular is your old standby. Jumbo is bigger, and mini is for tiny little dishes, like mini muffins or appetizers. You'll need all three sizes if you plan to try all the recipes in this book. Be aware that different manufacturers make their tins in slightly different sizes; so while a recipe in this book may be for 12 regular muffin cups, if yours is a bit smaller, you might find that your recipe stretches to 13 cups.

A newcomer on the muffin tin scene is the square muffin pan. These pans usually have 12 square cups that are a bit larger than regular round muffin cups (they hold slightly less than ¾ cup, while regular round cups hold about ½ cup). They're great for making things like brownies, little cakes, and little loaves of bread, or just to change things up.

Not only do muffin tins come in different diameters, but they also come with different numbers of actual cups in them. The most common are 6, 12, and 24 cups per pan. Any configuration will work, but smaller numbers of cups may mean you will need to bake in batches for the larger recipes.

Each recipe indicates the size of muffin tin needed; you'll find this to the right of the recipe yield next to the muffin icon.

Keep in mind that you can make your dishes any size you like, but you will need to adjust cooking time up or down accordingly (if you make a bigger cup than the recipe suggests, baking time will be longer; if you make a smaller cup, baking time will be shortened).

Muffin Pan Liners

Some of these recipes are cooked directly in the tin, while others require liners. There are more types of muffin tin liners available now than you could even imagine. The old standby is the paper liner, but you can find these now in many colors (and patterns), as well as in a parchment version that has more nonstick properties. Foil liners are a paper liner fitted inside a foil liner. It's important to keep the paper liners inside the foil liners when using them. The paper keeps the muffin cup from losing moisture, and the foil keeps everything together.

You can also buy individual reusable silicone muffin liners. They come in all the colors of the rainbow. These pop into your metal muffin tin and are removed like paper liners, or you can just set them on a baking sheet (note though that if you do this, your recipe will cook faster than if you put the liners in the tins). If you're only making 4 muffin cups, you can use exactly 4 silicone cups on a baking sheet, unlike regular muffin tins where you use the entire pan no matter how many cups you fill. You need to wash silicone liners to be able to reuse them (they are dishwasher safe). Their reusability is one benefit. Another is their firmness, which holds food in better. This is particularly helpful if you're serving the food right in the cup (as many recipes in this book do).

Tulip muffin liners (paper liners that have tall points sticking up from them into the air) are very pretty and work best for things like cupcakes and muffins. They aren't very practical for the other types of foods in this cookbook.

One thing to note about muffin tin liners is that they tend to vary slightly in size from brand to brand. Some may be slightly smaller than the openings in your muffin pan, while others might be slightly larger (and will need to be gently pressed in to fit). If your muffin liners are a slightly different size from your tin, it can change the amount that a recipe makes, so just be aware of this as you cook. You might need to make one more cup if your liners are slightly smaller.

Using Pie Crusts

Many recipes in this book use pie crusts. These recipes refer you back to this page for instructions on how to cut out the crusts.

Unroll your refrigerated pie crust (you can make your own if you prefer; if you do, be sure to roll it out to about a 9" circle). Align a 4" biscuit cutter (or a 28-ounce can of tomatoes is exactly the right size) against the edge of the crust. Cut out 1 circle. Repeat, cutting the next as close as possible to the previous cut-out. You will get 5 circles. Now take 2 big pieces of dough and press them together so you can cut out 1 more circle. Place each circle into a regular muffin tin cup. It will fit exactly, so the edge of the crust is right at the top edge of the cup.

Crescent Roll Crusts

Some recipes in the book use crescent roll dough as crusts. Open up the tube of crescent roll dough and separate the pieces into individual triangles. Take one triangle and place the shortest side (the one that is opposite the point) in the bottom of the cup. Fold the rest of the dough around into the cup, then press the dough around until it completely lines the inside of the cup and the edges meet.

Baking Times

Note that the baking times in this book have been tested, but your oven may vary. Always check on your food a few minutes before it should be done, to be sure. Don't be afraid to add a few minutes to your baking time if something does not appear completely done. Be sure to test meats for the temperatures recommended by the USDA:

MEAT TEMPERATURE CHART	
MEAT	Temperature
ALL WHOLE CUTS OF MEAT, INCLUDING PORK	145°F
GROUND BEEF, PORK, AND LAMB	160°F
ALL POULTRY	165°F

Serving

It is always a good idea to let your baked muffin cups rest for a few minutes before attempting to remove them from the tin. Mini pies especially need some time to rest and cool off before removing. If your recipe is made in a muffin liner, serve it in the liner, removed from the tin. If it is made directly in the tin, remove it from the tin for plating or serving. When removing items cooked directly in the tins, carefully run a thin knife around the edges to loosen them. Then use a knife, fork, or thin spoon to lift them out. This same technique will work for removing items made in liners; use a spoon and get it underneath the bottom of the liner to lift.

Dishes created in muffin cups look very pretty arranged or stacked on a platter, but they can also be directly plated. Another fun serving idea is to buy a cupcake tree or stand, which holds finished cupcakes in layers and can be used for many muffin tin recipes. Test out any items before serving them in the wire trees; some of the dishes in this book that are not solid enough (a vegetable dish, for example) might slip through the wire holder.

Nutritional Analysis

The recipes in this book are complete with full nutrition data. You'll see a listing that looks like this:

CALORIES	97 calories
FAT	2.2 grams
PROTEIN	3.8 grams
SODIUM	74 mg
CARBOHYDRATES	15.5 grams
SUGARS	1.4 grams
FIBER	1.5 grams

That means that particular recipe has 97 calories, 2.2 grams of fat, 3.8 grams of protein, 74 milligrams of sodium, 15.5 grams of carbohydrates, 1.4 grams of sugars, and 1.5 grams of fiber per piece. Nutrition information does not include optional ingredients.

Recipes that the cookbook's nutritionist has identified as healthy are listed with a ✿ icon next to the recipe title. A recipe is considered healthy if it is low in saturated fat and sodium. Usually, only foods with no more than 30 percent of calories from fat are identified as healthy, but some recipes that have a higher fat content have been labeled "healthy" because some of the fat comes from nuts or olive oil, which are heart-healthy fats. For healthy recipes, sodium per serving is under 500 mg. To keep sodium content down, you can also choose not to add salt to any of the recipes, and substitute lower-sodium versions of sauces and condiments. It's important to remember balance and to look at the overall picture when choosing recipes; a vegetable recipe with lots of cheese (high in saturated fat and sodium) will not be as healthy as a vegetable recipe that uses olive oil or has no added fat. Muffin tin cooking is a fun way to try old favorites and new flavors. Enjoy your muffin tin adventures!

Chapter 1

Appetizers and Snacks

Whether you're making an appetizer for a party, a snack for yourself or your family, or just want to make something fun and small, muffin tins are a terrific way to cook. Not only can you make perfectly portioned appetizers and snacks, you can also create perfectly shaped bites as well.

shrimp cakes with cilantro lime dipping sauce

Makes 12

 Mini

8 ounces raw shrimp, peeled
½ the green part of a scallion
⅛ stalk of celery
⅛ teaspoon dry mustard
¾ teaspoon lemon juice
3 tablespoons panko
1 egg white
1 tablespoon light mayonnaise
Salt and pepper to taste
Pinch of Old Bay seasoning

1. Preheat the oven to 350°F.

2. Fill 12 mini muffin cups with paper liners and spray them with cooking spray.

3. Place all ingredients in a food processor and pulse until the vegetables are completely chopped and the ingredients are completely mixed. If you do not have a food processor, finely chop shrimp, scallion, and celery. Mix with the other ingredients in a small bowl.

4. Fill each cup to the top.

5. Bake for 9 minutes, until the cakes are set and the shrimp cooked through.

Dipping sauce:

Mix ½ cup light mayonnaise, 2 tablespoons chopped cilantro and 1 tablespoon lime juice in a small bowl. Serve as a dipping sauce or place a dollop on top of each shrimp cake.

You can also make this recipe in a regular muffin tin and serve it on a bun with the mayo sauce as a shrimp burger.

CALORIES	20 calories
FAT	0.5 gram
PROTEIN	2.8 grams
SODIUM	115 mg
CARBOHYDRATES	1 gram
SUGARS	0.13 gram
FIBER	0 grams

stuffed mushrooms

Makes 12–20, depending on mushroom size Mini

10 ounces baby bella or white mushrooms, stems removed and reserved
¼ cup seasoned bread crumbs
1 tablespoon light cream cheese
Salt and pepper
1 tablespoon grated Parmesan cheese, plus additional for topping
Pinch dry mustard
½ teaspoon Italian seasoning
½ small garlic clove
1 tablespoon shredded part-skim mozzarella cheese
2 tablespoons grated fontina cheese
1 tablespoon olive oil
1 tablespoon melted unsalted butter
1 tablespoon frozen spinach, defrosted and squeezed dry

1. Preheat oven to 400°F, and prepare as many mini muffin cups as you have mushrooms (since sizes vary) by spraying with cooking spray.

2. Place one mushroom cap in each muffin cup.

3. Place remaining ingredients and 4 mushroom stems in food processor and pulse until completely mixed.

4. Divide mixture among the mushroom caps.

5. Cover with foil and bake 20 minutes, until mushrooms are cooked through.

6. Remove from oven, remove foil, and sprinkle a large pinch of Parmesan cheese on top of each cap.

7. Return to oven uncovered, and bake for 5 more minutes. Serve.

This recipe is a great way to make stuffed mushrooms because the caps don't slide around. The muffin cups hold them in place. Add 1 slice chopped cooked bacon to the stuffing, for some additional flavor.

CALORIES	53 calories (for 12-serving batch)
FAT	3.5 grams
PROTEIN	2.6 grams
SODIUM	73 mg
CARBOHYDRATES	2.8 grams
SUGARS	0.75 gram
FIBER	0.4 gram

corn chip nachos

Makes 8

 Jumbo

½ pound lean ground beef
½ cup salsa (your choice of heat)
2 cups Fritos, plus additional for topping
1 cup shredded taco cheese
4 teaspoons chopped green chilies

1. Preheat oven to 400°F, and prepare 8 jumbo muffin cups with foil or silicone liners.

2. Cook beef in a pan, until browned.

3. Stir in salsa, and cook until reduced.

4. Place ¼ cup Fritos in each cup.

5. Top with 1 tablespoon cheese in each cup.

6. Top with beef, divided among cups.

7. Top with 7 or 8 Fritos in each cup.

8. Sprinkle 1 tablespoon cheese on each.

9. Top with ½ teaspoon chilies on each.

10. Bake for 5 minutes, or until the cheese is melted.

I love having individual servings of this snack. These fun treats are easiest to eat with a fork, but fingers are definitely allowed. Try some for your next Super Bowl party!

CALORIES	180 calories
FAT	10 grams
PROTEIN	16 grams
SODIUM	369 mg
CARBOHYDRATES	6 grams
SUGARS	0.2 gram
FIBER	0.2 gram

scallop bites

Makes 12

 Mini

12 sea scallops, washed, cleaned, and dried
1 garlic clove, chopped
¼ teaspoon grated fresh gingerroot
2 teaspoons lime juice
2 tablespoons olive oil
1 teaspoon tamari sauce (or soy sauce)
Salt and pepper, to taste

1. Preheat oven to 400°F, and prepare a 12-cup mini muffin tin by spraying it with cooking spray.

2. Place 1 scallop in each cup.

3. Mix other ingredients and spoon over the scallops.

4. Bake for 4–5 minutes, until the scallops are cooked through. Serve these yummy little bites on a plate of lettuce with a toothpick in each.

Sea scallops are the larger scallops and are used in this recipe. Bay scallops are the tiny scallops and don't work as well in this recipe because they cook too quickly.

CALORIES	35 calories
FAT	2.3 grams
PROTEIN	2.6 grams
SODIUM	111 mg
CARBOHYDRATES	1 gram
SUGARS	0 grams
FIBER	0 grams

savory cheesecakes

Makes 24

 Mini

½ cup seasoned bread crumbs
2 tablespoons melted unsalted butter
1 8-ounce package light cream cheese
1 egg
½ cup grated Gruyère cheese
1 teaspoon Dijon mustard
½ cup grated Parmesan cheese
¼ teaspoon paprika
Salt and pepper
½ 10-ounce package of frozen chopped spinach, defrosted and squeezed dry
Green part of 1 scallion, chopped

1. Preheat oven to 350°F, and prepare 24 mini muffin cups by spraying with cooking spray.

2. Mix bread crumbs and unsalted butter and then press into bottoms of muffin tins.

3. Mix all other ingredients in a bowl and divide among muffin tins.

4. Bake for 20 minutes until set and slightly brown and serve warm.

Great leftover idea: These are good reheated and crumbled over salads the next day.

CALORIES	62 calories
FAT	4 grams
PROTEIN	3.3 grams
SODIUM	159 mg
CARBOHYDRATES	3 grams
SUGARS	0.8 gram
FIBER	0.4 gram

cocktail meatballs

 Mini

Makes 12

½ pound lean ground beef
¼ cup seasoned bread crumbs
Salt and pepper
1 egg
¼ teaspoon onion powder
¼ teaspoon Italian seasoning
¼ cup bottled chili sauce
1¼ cups grape jelly

1. Preheat oven to 350°F, and prepare 12 mini muffin cups with foil liners.

2. Mix beef, bread crumbs, salt, pepper, egg, onion powder, and Italian seasoning in a bowl.

3. Shape into 12 small meatballs and place one in each cup.

4. Bake for 10 minutes until meat is cooked through.

5. Mix chili sauce and grape jelly together.

6. Spoon over meatballs and return to oven for about 10 more minutes, until bubbly.

7. Serve with toothpicks.

You can substitute lean ground turkey for the ground beef, but add 1 teaspoon olive oil if you do so to keep the meatballs moist.

CALORIES	144 calories
FAT	2.9 grams
PROTEIN	4.5 grams
SODIUM	135 mg
CARBOHYDRATES	24.4 grams
SUGARS	22.4 grams
FIBER	0.4 gram

asian dumplings with dipping sauce

Makes 24

 Mini

1 pound ground 99-percent-lean
   turkey
2 scallions, chopped finely
2 teaspoons minced lemongrass
½ teaspoon grated fresh
   gingerroot
Ground pepper, to taste
1 tablespoon tamari sauce (or
   soy sauce)
1 garlic clove, finely chopped
1 package of 24 wonton
   wrappers

Dipping Sauce
1 tablespoon rice vinegar
¼ cup tamari or soy sauce
2 tablespoons water
Green part of 1 scallion, minced
1 tablespoon sherry
1 teaspoon sesame oil

1. Preheat oven to 400°F, and prepare two 24-cup mini muffin pans by spraying every other muffin cup with cooking spray.

2. In a bowl, combine all the ingredients except wonton wrappers, and mix completely.

3. Brush the wrappers with water.

4. Place a wonton wrapper in the sprayed muffin cup and add about 1 tablespoon of filling.

5. Fold the edges of the wrapper into the center and gently press them down.

6. Repeat.

7. Brush the top of the dumplings with water.

8. Fill the empty cups halfway with boiling water.

9. Cover the muffin pans with foil and bake for 10 minutes.

10. Remove the foil, and spray the top of the dumplings with cooking spray.

11. Broil for 2–3 minutes, until golden brown on top.

12. Serve with dipping sauce.

Dipping Sauce

1. Mix and serve in a small bowl.

You can find wonton wrappers refrigerated or frozen at your grocery store. Be sure to buy the square wonton wrappers, not the rectangular eggroll wrappers.

CALORIES	44 calories (including dipping sauce)
FAT	0.5 gram
PROTEIN	7 grams
SODIUM	244 mg
CARBOHYDRATES	2.75 grams
SUGARS	0.1 gram
FIBER	0.15 gram

spiral snacks

Makes 16

 Mini

2 whole wheat tortillas
2 tablespoons pesto
8 slices provolone cheese
8 slices prosciutto

1. Preheat the oven to 400°F and prepare 16 mini muffin cups with foil or silicone liners, then spray the liners with cooking spray.

2. Lay the tortillas flat and spread each with half the pesto.

3. Lay 4 cheese slices on each, arranging to get as much coverage as you can, then do the same with the prosciutto.

4. Roll the tortillas and place seam side down.

5. Cut the ends off and discard, then slice the tortilla rolls into 1" pieces, resulting in about 8 pieces per tortilla.

6. Place each piece, cut side down, in a muffin cup. Bake for 8 minutes, until cheese is melted.

Use any cheese you like in this recipe. Try salami instead of prosciutto. No pesto? A little mustard will work instead.

CALORIES	80 calories
FAT	3.6 grams
PROTEIN	7.7 grams
SODIUM	486 mg
CARBOHYDRATES	4.2 grams
SUGARS	0.4 gram
FIBER	0.4 gram

smoked salmon cups

Makes 12

 Mini

12 ready-to-serve mini phyllo cups

12 1" × 1" squares of smoked salmon

1 4.4-ounce container of light Boursin cheese

24 pieces of fresh chives, each 1" long

1. Preheat the oven to 350°F, and prepare a 12-cup mini muffin tin.

2. Place a phyllo cup in each muffin cup.

3. Place 1 piece salmon at the bottom of each cup.

4. Top with the cheese (using about 1 teaspoon per cup).

5. Top with two 1" pieces of chive, crossed.

6. Bake for 8 minutes until the phyllo is lightly browned.

Phyllo cups can be found in the freezer section of your grocery store. Boursin is a cheese spread that comes in a plastic container. Look for it in the gourmet cheese section of your store.

CALORIES	42 calories
FAT	2.5 grams
PROTEIN	2.6 grams
SODIUM	344 mg
CARBOHYDRATES	2.3 grams
SUGARS	0 grams
FIBER	0 grams

hot pretzel bites

Makes 9

 Mini

2 frozen hot pretzels, thawed and broken into several pieces each

4 tablespoons spreadable light cream cheese

2 tablespoons shredded sharp white cheddar cheese

⅛ teaspoon of salt from the pretzel package

1 tablespoon chopped fresh chives

1 tablespoon cream

⅛ teaspoon dry mustard

1. Preheat oven to 400°F and prepare 9 mini muffin cups by spraying with cooking spray.

2. Place all ingredients in food processor and process until it resembles coarse dough.

3. Divide the dough among muffin cups, pressing down firmly.

4. Bake for about 11 minutes until the edges are a deep golden brown.

This dish takes hot pretzels to a new and elegant level. Serve these at a party instead of a basket of dry pretzels.

CALORIES	118 calories
FAT	3.2 grams
PROTEIN	3.5 grams
SODIUM	260 mg
CARBOHYDRATES	18.8 grams
SUGARS	0.5 gram
FIBER	0.5 gram

potato bites

Makes 24

 Mini

4 slices prosciutto
12 baby red potatoes, cooked (in the microwave) and cut in half
¼ cup crème fraiche
2 tablespoons blue cheese
Small bunch of chives, cut into 1" pieces

1. Preheat oven to 400°F, and prepare 24 mini muffin cups by spraying with cooking spray.

2. Lay the prosciutto slices on a greased baking sheet, and bake for about 5 minutes, until brown and crunchy.

3. Scoop about ½ to 1 teaspoon out of the center of each potato half.

4. Mix crème fraiche and blue cheese in a small bowl.

5. Fill the holes with the crème fraiche and blue cheese mixture.

6. Break the prosciutto into pieces, and top the potatoes with it.

7. Lay a few pieces of chive on top of each potato and place one potato half in each cup.

8. Bake for about 8–10 minutes, until heated through.

Crème fraiche is similar to sour cream but is thicker, with more fat and less sourness. You can substitute sour cream in a pinch.

CALORIES	50 calories
FAT	2 grams
PROTEIN	1.2 grams
SODIUM	17 mg
CARBOHYDRATES	7 grams
SUGARS	0.5 gram
FIBER	0.7 gram

spiced pecan cups

Makes 8

 Mini

1 cup pecan halves
2 tablespoons melted unsalted
    butter
2 teaspoons brown sugar
½ teaspoon salt
Pinch of ground pepper
⅛ teaspoon nutmeg

1. Preheat oven to 350°F and prepare a mini muffin tin with 8 foil liners.

2. Place the nuts in a bowl and add the other ingredients, stirring until completely mixed.

3. Divide among muffin cups and bake for 15 minutes.

These delicious spiced nuts are the perfect treat to set out at a holiday party. Each guest can just grab a mini cupcake liner full of nuts, and enjoy.

CALORIES	115 calories
FAT	11 grams
PROTEIN	1.2 grams
SODIUM	145 mg
CARBOHYDRATES	2.9 grams
SUGARS	1.6 grams
FIBER	1.2 grams

smoky popcorn cheese snacks

Makes 6

 Jumbo

5 cups popped popcorn
2 tablespoons melted unsalted
    butter
⅛ teaspoon salt
¼ cup grated Parmesan cheese
¼ cup shredded cheddar cheese
½ teaspoon smoked paprika

1. Preheat oven to 350°F and prepare 6 jumbo muffin cups with paper liners, sprayed with cooking spray.

2. Toss popcorn and other ingredients in a bowl, then divide among the muffin cups.

3. Bake for 5 minutes, or until cheese has melted.

This is a huge favorite at my house, where we love to make our own popcorn and flavor it in different ways. You can find smoked paprika in the spice aisle of your grocery store or at www.penzeys.com.

CALORIES	96 calories
FAT	6.4 grams
PROTEIN	3.7 grams
SODIUM	142 mg
CARBOHYDRATES	5.4 grams
SUGARS	0 grams
FIBER	1 gram

mushroom stuffed brie en croute

Makes 6

 Regular

1 sheet frozen puff pastry, thawed
4 ounces baby bella mushrooms, chopped
1 tablespoon olive oil
Salt and pepper
6 1"×1" squares of Brie

1. Preheat oven to 400°F and prepare 6 cups in a regular muffin tin.

2. Follow the instructions for pie crust (see "Using Pie Crusts" in the Introduction) but use a sheet of puff pastry, reserving the scraps.

3. Cook the mushrooms with the oil and salt and pepper over medium heat until they are softened and cooked down, about 5 minutes.

4. Take each square of brie and break it into 2 or 3 pieces, placing them in the bottom of the muffin cups lined with puff pastry.

5. Divide the mushrooms among the cups.

6. Divide the puff pastry scraps among the tops of the cups, not covering them completely.

7. Bake for 15 minutes until brown and puffy.

Serve these individual snacks instead of a big wheel of Brie at a party. They're delicious with grapes or sliced apples and pears.

CALORIES	160 calories
FAT	12.5 grams
PROTEIN	6.9 grams
SODIUM	247 mg
CARBOHYDRATES	4.4 grams
SUGARS	0.7 gram
FIBER	0.4 gram

shrimp toasts

Makes 24

Mini

12 slices of bread, your preference
8 ounces raw shrimp (peeled)
½ of the green part of a scallion
¼ teaspoon paprika
2 tablespoons light mayonnaise
1 tablespoon lemon juice
¼ teaspoon salt
⅛ teaspoon ground pepper
¼ teaspoon dry mustard
¼ teaspoon garlic powder
⅛ teaspoon cayenne pepper
¼ teaspoon dried dill weed
½ teaspoon baking powder

1. Preheat oven to 400°F and prepare 24 mini muffin cups by spraying with cooking spray.

2. Remove crusts from bread and cut each piece in half.

3. Take each half and press it into a muffin cup, along the bottom and up the side, pressing it tight against the pan.

4. Spray the bread with cooking spray, and bake for about 12 minutes until golden brown.

5. Place all other ingredients in a food processor and pulse until completely pulverized.

6. Divide among muffin cups, then bake for 10 minutes. Serve warm.

My parents always served deep-fried shrimp toasts at their yearly Christmas party. This version is lower in fat and easier to make. You can make this with any type of bread you like; change it up by using different varieties.

CALORIES	49 calories
FAT	0.8 gram
PROTEIN	2.5 grams
SODIUM	173 mg
CARBOHYDRATES	7.9 grams
SUGARS	0.7 gram
FIBER	0.4 gram

spinach artichoke dip cups

Makes 9

 Regular

1 cup frozen artichoke heart quarters, thawed
5 ounces frozen chopped spinach, defrosted and squeezed dry
½ cup plain low-fat or fat-free yogurt
2 ounces light cream cheese
1 tablespoon lemon juice
1 clove garlic
¼ teaspoon ground red pepper
½ cup shredded fontina cheese
½ cup grated Parmesan or Romano cheese
⅛ teaspoon ground black pepper
¼ teaspoon salt
1 tablespoon light mayonnaise
¼ cup smoked Gouda
Crackers, toast points, or toasted pita triangles, for serving

1. Preheat oven to 400°F and prepare 9 regular size muffin cups with silicone liners, sprayed with cooking spray.

2. Place all ingredients (except crackers) in food processor and process until completely puréed and combined.

3. Divide among muffin cups and bake for 15 minutes. Serve with crackers, toast points, or toasted pita triangles.

This recipe lends itself well to some tinkering with the cheeses. Try it with Asiago instead of the smoked Gouda. Dip is so convenient when served in muffin cups. Everyone gets their own, and there's no fear of double dipping.

CALORIES	98 calories (dip only)
FAT	5.8 grams
PROTEIN	6.8 grams
SODIUM	33 mg
CARBOHYDRATES	4.5 grams
SUGARS	1.7 grams
FIBER	1.3 grams

sausage in kluski noodle cups

Makes 21

 Mini

1½ cups kluski noodles, cooked according to package instructions
1 tablespoon cream
Salt and pepper, to taste
1 garlic and herb chicken sausage
¼ cup chopped escarole (or chopped endive)
2 ounces light cream cheese
¼ cup plain Greek-style low-fat or fat-free yogurt

1. Preheat oven to 400°F and prepare 21 mini muffin cups by spraying with cooking spray.

2. Place noodles, cream, and salt and pepper in food processor and process until noodles are finely chopped and a paste forms.

3. Divide noodle mix among cups, placing about 1 tablespoon in each. Press to cover the bottoms and sides.

4. Wash out the food processor, then place remaining ingredients in it and process until completely combined.

5. Divide among cups.

6. Bake for 18 minutes until heated through and slightly bubbly and browned.

Kluski noodles are a type of egg noodle that you can find in your grocery store's pasta aisle. They make these noodle cups delicious! Try these cups with other fillings, such as cheese or roasted vegetables.

CALORIES	35 calories
FAT	1.2 grams
PROTEIN	2 grams
SODIUM	67 mg
CARBOHYDRATES	4.1 grams
SUGARS	0.4 gram
FIBER	0.2 gram

hot nuts

Makes 9

Mini

1½ cups mixed nuts
1 tablespoon melted unsalted butter
¼ cup Asian sweet chili sauce

1. Preheat oven to 400°F and prepare 9 mini muffin cups with foil or silicone liners.

2. Mix all ingredients in a bowl then divide among muffin cups.

3. Bake for 10 minutes until nuts are shiny and slightly darkened in color.

This is a terrific holiday party food item that will impress your guests. They'll never realize how incredibly simple it is to make. Shh . . . you don't have to tell!

CALORIES	163 calories
FAT	12.4 grams
PROTEIN	4 grams
SODIUM	199 mg
CARBOHYDRATES	8.9 grams
SUGARS	3.7 grams
FIBER	2 grams

crab dip cups

Makes 9

 Regular

1 cup lump crabmeat, picked
   over
6 ounces light cream cheese
½ teaspoon onion powder
1 teaspoon Worcestershire sauce
1 tablespoon chopped fresh
   parsley
2 teaspoons prepared
   horseradish
1 tablespoon skim milk
Green part of 1 scallion,
   chopped
¼ cup slivered toasted almonds,
   coarsely chopped
2 teaspoons lemon juice
2 tablespoons light mayonnaise
1 tablespoon sherry
⅛ teaspoon paprika
⅛ teaspoon garlic powder
¼ teaspoon Old Bay seasoning
Crackers, toast points, or toasted
   pita triangles, for serving

1. Preheat oven to 400°F and prepare 9 regular muffin cups with silicone liners. Spray liners with cooking spray.

2. Mix all ingredients together (except crackers) and divide among muffin cups.

3. Bake for 12–15 minutes, until bubbly. Serve with crackers, toast points, or toasted pita triangles.

Be sure to use real, not imitation, crabmeat in this recipe. If fresh isn't available, frozen or canned will also do.

CALORIES	81 calories (dip only)
FAT	5.1 grams
PROTEIN	5 grams
SODIUM	187 mg
CARBOHYDRATES	3.2 grams
SUGARS	1.7 grams
FIBER	0.5 gram

cheese coins

Makes 24

 Mini

1 cup flour
7 tablespoons unsalted butter
¼ teaspoon baking powder
⅛ teaspoon pepper
Pinch cayenne pepper
½ teaspoon salt
1 egg, separated
½ cup shredded Asiago cheese
½ cup shredded Romano cheese
¼ cup shredded cheddar cheese

1. Preheat oven to 400°F and prepare 24 mini muffin cups by spraying with cooking spray.

2. Place flour, butter, baking powder, pepper, cayenne, and salt in the food processor and combine until it resembles coarse meal.

3. Add egg white and cheeses and pulse until dough forms.

4. Divide dough among the bottom of the muffin tins and press to make a coin shape.

5. Mix egg yolk with 1 tablespoon water and brush the tops of the coins.

6. Bake for 15 minutes until golden brown around the edges.

Try substituting ¼ cup blue cheese for ¼ cup of the cheddar cheese for a different flavor. These coins keep and reheat well, so you can make them in advance for a party.

CALORIES	69 calories
FAT	4.7 grams
PROTEIN	2.1 grams
SODIUM	104 mg
CARBOHYDRATES	4.1 grams
SUGARS	0 grams
FIBER	0.1 gram

Chapter 2

Breakfast

Muffin tins will revolutionize the way you make breakfast. No more standing over a stove, stirring and flipping! Eggs cook beautifully in muffin tins as do ham and sausage. Starting your morning with a lovely little breakfast completely contained in a muffin cup is a wonderful beginning to the day. Many of these recipes can be assembled the night before and refrigerated until you're ready to pop them in the oven. Be sure to check Chapter 8, Muffins and Breads, for other breakfast ideas, since muffins also make great breakfasts.

egg crescent pockets

Makes 8

1 package of 8 crescent rolls dough
4 large slices of deli ham, cut in half
½ cup herbed goat cheese (or cheese of your choice)
Dried thyme, to taste
8 eggs
Salt and pepper

1. Preheat oven to 375°F.

2. Place 8 muffin cup liners in a regular muffin tin and spray the inside of them with cooking spray.

3. Follow the instructions for crescent roll dough in "Crescent Roll Crusts" in the Introduction.

4. Take half a piece of ham and fold it so it fits inside the liner.

5. Place the goat cheese on top of the ham, and add a pinch of thyme.

6. Crack an egg and place it in the liner.

7. Sprinkle with salt and pepper to taste.

8. Bake for 20 minutes, until egg whites are completely set and crescent rolls are browned. Allow each to rest for a few minutes before lifting the cups out of the muffin pan.

Try this with salami instead of ham and provolone instead of goat cheese, for a different flavor. This is great with some fruit salad at brunch.

CALORIES	245 calories
FAT	15.5 grams
PROTEIN	13.7 grams
SODIUM	619 mg
CARBOHYDRATES	12.3 grams
SUGARS	3.5 grams
FIBER	0.2 gram

french bread french toast

Makes 18–23 (depending on the length of the baguette) Regular

1 fresh baguette, ends cut off
   and sliced into 1" slices
6 eggs
½ cup skim milk
½ cup heavy cream
½ teaspoon cinnamon

1. Preheat oven to 400°F and prepare as many regular muffin cups as you have slices of bread by spraying with cooking spray.

2. Whisk all other ingredients together in a bowl.

3. Drop 5 or 6 slices of bread into the bowl, and allow them to soak for about 30 seconds, flipping halfway through.

4. Place 1 slice in each muffin cup. Repeat process for remaining slices.

5. Divide any remaining egg mixture among the muffin cups evenly by spooning over the top of the toast.

6. Bake for 12–15 minutes, rotating muffin pans halfway through, until lightly browned.

Perfect for when you've got a big crowd for breakfast, this recipe lets you make all the French toast at once in the oven. Serve with maple syrup, jam, powdered sugar, or apple butter.

CALORIES	141 calories (for 18 servings)
FAT	4.3 grams
PROTEIN	6.2 grams
SODIUM	193 mg
CARBOHYDRATES	18.8 grams
SUGARS	1.2 grams
FIBER	0.8 gram

bagel sausage sandwiches

Makes 2

 Jumbo

2 mini bagels, halved
2 tablespoons goat cheese
1 chicken sausage, removed
   from casing
2 slices tomato, seeded
1 slice Swiss cheese

1. Preheat oven to 400°F, and prepare 2 jumbo muffin cups with paper liners.

2. Spread the goat cheese on the bagel halves and place one half, cheese side up, in each tin.

3. Crumble the sausage on top, pressing into the goat cheese.

4. Place 1 tomato slice on top of each.

5. Break the Swiss cheese into 4 quarters and place 2 on each sandwich. Top with remaining bagel halves.

6. Bake for 15 minutes or until bagel is slightly browned and filling is hot.

This dish is easy to make and take with you for breakfast-on-the-go. For ultimate portability, take it out of the pan (keep in its paper liner) and wrap in waxed paper or parchment paper.

CALORIES	244 calories
FAT	11.6 grams
PROTEIN	18.2 grams
SODIUM	493 mg
CARBOHYDRATES	15.6 grams
SUGARS	1.1 grams
FIBER	0.8 gram

grits casserole

Makes 12

 Regular

½ cup dry uncooked grits
¼ cup heavy cream
2 eggs
½ small onion, chopped
5 button mushrooms, thinly sliced
1 tablespoon butter
6 fresh breakfast link sausages,
    removed from casing
½ teaspoon salt
Ground pepper, to taste
½ cup shredded Muenster
    cheese
¼ teaspoon dry mustard

1. Cook grits according to package instructions.

2. Preheat oven to 375°F, and prepare 12 regular muffin cups with foil or silicone liners.

3. Mix cream and eggs. Stir a few tablespoons of hot grits into the cream-and-eggs mixture to temper it, then stir the cream-and-eggs mixture into the remaining grits.

4. In a skillet over medium-high heat, cook onion and mushrooms in the butter, until mushrooms cook down and are soft.

5. Add sausage to mushroom mix and cook, stirring to break up the sausage, until it is cooked through.

6. Add sausage-mushroom mixture to grits. Salt and pepper to taste.

7. Stir in cheese and dry mustard, then divide among muffin cups.

8. Bake for about 23 minutes, until the cups are set and turning lightly brown on top.

Serve this with half a grapefruit, and you've got a complete breakfast. For a different taste, try various types of sausages.

CALORIES	86 calories
FAT	6.7 grams
PROTEIN	3.6 grams
SODIUM	219 mg
CARBOHYDRATES	1.8 grams
SUGARS	0.5 gram
FIBER	0.2 gram

cheese danish cups

Maker 8

 Regular

1 tube refrigerated crescent roll
    dough (8 pieces)
8 ounces light cream cheese
¼ cup powdered sugar
½ teaspoon vanilla
1 egg yolk
4–6 tablespoons strawberry jam

1. Preheat oven to 400°F, and prepare 8 regular muffin cups.

2. Place one crescent roll in each cup, with the thin pointy side of the triangle coming out of the cup and the opposite side in the bottom of the cup. Then wrap and tuck the long pointy end around the sides of the cup, pressing it and the bottom edge so the entire cup is lined.

3. Mix cream cheese, sugar, vanilla, and egg yolk, until completely combined.

4. Divide cream cheese mixture among cups and use your thumb or a spoon to create a big indent in the middle of each.

5. Place about ½ to ¾ tablespoon strawberry jam in each indentation.

6. Bake for 10–12 minutes, until filling is set and roll is golden brown.

Who knew making Danish could be so incredibly simple? Try it with different flavors of jams.

CALORIES	213 calories
FAT	10.5 grams
PROTEIN	4.6 grams
SODIUM	358 mg
CARBOHYDRATES	25.6 grams
SUGARS	14.3 grams
FIBER	0.1 gram

ham and egg cups

Makes 1

 Regular

1 slice round or oval deli ham
1 egg
Salt and pepper, to taste
½ tablespoon shaved Parmesan
   cheese

1. Preheat the oven to 400°F.

2. Prepare 1 regular muffin cup by spraying it or using a muffin cup liner.

3. Place the center of the ham into the middle of the cup, and arrange the edges along the inside of the cup. If it sticks up a bit above the cup, that's fine.

4. Crack the egg, and place it inside the ham.

5. Season with salt and pepper, and add the cheese.

6. Bake for 15 minutes, until the white of the egg is set.

Using the ham as a cup is a really fun way to serve eggs, and it makes an especially good breakfast for those on a low-carb diet.

CALORIES	126 calories
FAT	7.3 grams
PROTEIN	11.9 grams
SODIUM	474 mg
CARBOHYDRATES	1.5 grams
SUGARS	0.2 gram
FIBER	0.4 gram

coffee cakes

Makes 10

 Regular

¾ cup flour
¾ cup whole wheat pastry flour
1½ teaspoons baking powder
½ cup sugar
¼ teaspoon salt
1 egg
4 tablespoons melted unsalted
  butter
⅔ cup buttermilk
1 tablespoon skim milk
¼ cup brown sugar
½ teaspoon cinnamon

1. Preheat oven to 350°F and prepare 10 regular muffin cups by spraying them with cooking spray or lining with paper liners.

2. Mix flours, baking powder, sugar, and salt in a bowl. In a separate bowl, mix together egg, melted butter, buttermilk, and skim milk and pour into dry ingredients, mixing well.

3. Divide batter among muffin cups, filling about ⅔ full.

4. Mix brown sugar and cinnamon in a small bowl then sprinkle on top of each muffin.

5. Bake about 13 minutes, until a cake tester comes out clean.

Spice yours up by adding 1 tablespoon ground nuts to the topping and/ or ¼ teaspoon nutmeg to the dry ingredients. These are best served warm, fresh from the oven with a cup of coffee or tea.

CALORIES	184 calories
FAT	5.3 grams
PROTEIN	3.2 grams
SODIUM	155 mg
CARBOHYDRATES	30.4 grams
SUGARS	16.3 grams
FIBER	1.2 grams

denver omelets

Makes 6

 Regular

4 eggs
¼ cup skim milk
Salt and pepper to taste
2 teaspoons chopped fresh
   chives
⅓ cup shredded cheddar, plus
   a few pinches reserved for
   topping
⅓ cup chopped prosciutto
1 tablespoon melted unsalted
   butter

1. Preheat oven to 350°F.

2. Prepare 6 regular muffin cups. You can cook directly in the cups (spray with cooking spray first) or use foil or silicone liners.

3. Place all ingredients in a bowl and use a fork or whisk to completely combine.

4. Divide among the muffin cups. An ice cream scoop will allow you to divide evenly and get all the ingredients in each scoop.

5. Sprinkle tops with remaining cheese.

6. Bake for 17 minutes until egg is completely cooked.

7. Allow to cool briefly before removing and serving.

Feel free to change up this recipe by substituting different ingredients in this dish. Use different herbs or cheeses, or use bacon or ham instead of prosciutto.

CALORIES	102 calories
FAT	7.4 grams
PROTEIN	6.7 grams
SODIUM	106 mg
CARBOHYDRATES	0.9 gram
SUGARS	0.7 gram
FIBER	0 grams

english muffin casserole

Makes 8

 Regular

3 whole wheat English muffins
3 uncooked breakfast sausage
 links removed from casings
2 eggs
Green part of 1 scallion,
 chopped
Salt and pepper
¼ cup shredded Monterey Jack
 cheese
¼ cup heavy cream
½ cup skim milk
Pinch cayenne pepper
⅛ teaspoon thyme
⅛ teaspoon onion powder

1. Preheat oven to 350°F, and prepare 8 regular muffin cups with foil or silicone liners, sprayed with cooking spray.

2. Tear the English muffins into 1" pieces and place in a bowl.

3. Add other ingredients, and completely combine (you may want to use your hands for this).

4. Divide among muffin cups, and bake for 20–22 minutes, until set and slightly browned.

English muffins add a different and fun texture to this breakfast casserole. You could also make this with ham instead of sausage.

CALORIES	129 calories
FAT	6.5 grams
PROTEIN	5.8 grams
SODIUM	215 mg
CARBOHYDRATES	11 grams
SUGARS	1.3 grams
FIBER	1.1 grams

granola bars

Makes 24

Mini

2 cups quick-cooking oats (uncooked)
1 tablespoon ground flaxseed
1 tablespoon wheat bran
¼ teaspoon salt
½ teaspoon vanilla
¼ cup brown sugar
¾ cup chopped nuts
¼ cup chopped dried fruit (such as apricots)
1 egg white
¼ cup real maple syrup (do not use "pancake syrup")
4 tablespoons unsalted butter, melted

1. Preheat oven to 400°F and prepare 24 mini muffin cups by spraying with cooking spray.

2. Mix all ingredients in a bowl, until combined.

3. Divide among muffin cups.

4. Bake for 12–13 minutes until browned around edges and not mushy in the middle.

Chewy, slightly crunchy, and very satisfying, these mini granola bars are wonderful for a breakfast-on-the-go or as a snack. Package them in snack-size zip-top bags for grab-and-go healthy snacks.

CALORIES	115 calories
FAT	4.8 grams
PROTEIN	3.2 grams
SODIUM	56 mg
CARBOHYDRATES	15 grams
SUGARS	4.3 grams
FIBER	2 grams

apple-granola yogurt cups

Makes 6

Regular

1 apple, peeled, cored, and chopped
½ cup granola
½ cup plain Greek-style low-fat or fat-free yogurt
½ teaspoon cinnamon
1 tablespoon honey or maple syrup

1. Preheat oven to 350°F and prepare 6 regular muffin cups with silicone or foil liners.

2. Mix all ingredients in a bowl, then divide among muffin cups.

3. Bake for 35 minutes until browned.

These are yummy served warm on a cold morning. Substitute regular plain low-fat or fat-free yogurt if you don't have Greek, but expect the end result to be a bit less thick.

CALORIES	68 calories
FAT	1 gram
PROTEIN	2.8 grams
SODIUM	11 mg
CARBOHYDRATES	13 grams
SUGARS	8.4 grams
FIBER	1 gram

corned beef hash cups

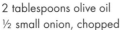 Makes 12

 Regular

2 tablespoons olive oil
½ small onion, chopped
3 cups refrigerator hash brown
    potatoes (chunks, not shreds)
Salt and pepper
½ teaspoon thyme
¼ pound sliced deli corned beef,
    chopped
12 eggs

1. Preheat oven to 350°F, and prepare 12 regular muffin cups with foil or silicone liners.

2. Heat a skillet over medium-high heat, and add olive oil and onions, then add potatoes.

3. Add salt and pepper and thyme, and cook, stirring occasionally, about 15 minutes.

4. Stir in corned beef and divide mixture among the cups, pressing down into the bottoms.

5. Place contents of 1 egg on top of each cup, and bake for 12 minutes, until whites are set.

This recipe calls for sliced deli corned beef, but if you happen to have leftover whole corned beef, you can use that. This recipe is a great way to use up corned beef leftovers from St. Patrick's Day.

CALORIES	159 calories
FAT	8.3 grams
PROTEIN	9.1 grams
SODIUM	213 mg
CARBOHYDRATES	10 grams
SUGARS	0.3 gram
FIBER	0.8 gram

breakfast sausage

Makes 12

 Regular

1 pound ground pork
1 tablespoon seasoned bread
   crumbs
⅛ teaspoon cinnamon
½ teaspoon dried parsley
¼ teaspoon dried rosemary
½ teaspoon dried sage
½ teaspoon dried thyme
¼ teaspoon onion powder
¼ teaspoon salt
⅛ teaspoon ground pepper

1. Preheat oven to 350°F, and prepare 12 regular muffin cups by spraying with cooking spray.

2. Mix all ingredients in a bowl, until completely combined.

3. Divide among muffin cups, pressing into the bottoms.

4. Bake for 15 minutes, until pork is cooked through. Refer to the "Meat Temperature Chart" in the Introduction for doneness.

Making your own breakfast sausage is so easy! Using fresh herbs instead of dried will make this dish more flavorful. These patties freeze well and can be reheated quickly for weekday breakfasts.

CALORIES	134 calories
FAT	9.8 grams
PROTEIN	8 grams
SODIUM	414 mg
CARBOHYDRATES	3.4 grams
SUGARS	0.3 gram
FIBER	0.3 gram

hardboiled eggs

Makes 12

 Regular

12 eggs

1. Preheat oven to 325°F.

2. Place 1 whole egg, still in the shell, in each section of a regular muffin tin.

3. Bake for 25 minutes.

4. Remove from muffin tin using tongs, and place in a bowl or sink of ice water, until cool.

5. You can store in the refrigerator for up to 1 week. Peel and serve.

Cooking hardboiled eggs in the oven in a muffin tin is a great solution when you need to make a lot, don't want to steam up the kitchen, or don't want to keep an eye on boiling water.

CALORIES	71 calories
FAT	4.4 grams
PROTEIN	6.3 grams
SODIUM	71 mg
CARBOHYDRATES	0.4 gram
SUGARS	0.2 gram
FIBER	0 grams

gram's mission coffee cake

Makes 12

 Regular

½ cup golden raisins
1 cup water
¼ cup unsalted butter
½ cup sugar
½ teaspoon cinnamon
½ teaspoon nutmeg
½ teaspoon baking soda
1 cup whole wheat pastry flour
½ teaspoon cloves
½ cup chopped nuts
⅛ teaspoon salt
Crumb topping (see Nectarine Crisp with Crumb Topping, in Chapter 9)

1. Preheat oven to 350°F.

2. Prepare 12 regular muffin cups with paper liners.

3. Place the raisins and water in a 4-cup glass measuring cup and microwave on high for 5 minutes.

4. Place the butter in a bowl and pour the raisins and water over it, allowing it to melt.

5. Add other ingredients, and stir until combined.

6. Divide among the muffin cups.

7. Place 1 tablespoon Crumb Topping on each.

8. Bake for 25 minutes, until a cake tester comes out clean.

Based on my grandmother's World War II recipe for a cake, this breakfast treat is filling and hearty. You can substitute regular raisins for golden raisins in this recipe.

CALORIES	207 calories
FAT	8.8 grams
PROTEIN	2.6 grams
SODIUM	125 mg
CARBOHYDRATES	30 grams
SUGARS	17.5 grams
FIBER	2.2 grams

eggs and lox

Makes 8

 Regular

2 ounces light cream cheese
4 eggs
2 tablespoons nonfat milk
Salt and pepper, to taste
1 tablespoon chopped fresh
  chives
¼ cup roughly chopped smoked
  salmon
Toasted bagels and orange
  juice, for serving

1. Preheat oven to 400°F, and prepare 8 regular muffin cups by spraying them well with cooking spray.

2. Place cream cheese in the freezer for about 15 minutes, to make it easy to cut.

3. Cut cream cheese into ¼" cubes.

4. Mix eggs, milk, salt, pepper, and chives. Stir in salmon and cream cheese.

5. Distribute among the muffin cups, filling each about halfway.

6. Bake for 10 minutes. Serve this delightful dish with some toasted bagels and orange juice.

To make fresh chives easy to chop, fold the bunch over several times and cut through them all. Kitchen shears are a great alternative to cutting them with a knife, and the folding method works for that as well.

CALORIES	120 calories
FAT	7.2 grams
PROTEIN	11.6 grams
SODIUM	566 mg
CARBOHYDRATES	1.9 grams
SUGARS	1.4 grams
FIBER	0 grams

baby dutch babies

Maker 10

 Jumbo

3 eggs
½ cup flour
½ cup skim milk
2 tablespoons melted unsalted
    butter
Pinch of salt
2 tablespoons butter, divided
2½ teaspoons lemon juice,
    divided
5 teaspoons powdered sugar,
    divided
10 strawberries, hulled and
    sliced
Maple syrup for serving

1. Preheat oven to 400°F, and prepare 10 jumbo muffin cups by spraying with cooking spray.

2. Mix eggs, milk, flour, melted butter, and salt in a medium bowl. The batter will be slightly lumpy.

3. Place 2 tablespoons of batter in each muffin cup.

4. Bake for 3 minutes. Open the oven, slide out the pans, and poke the center of each Dutch baby a few times with a fork.

5. Reduce temperature to 350°F and bake for another 5 minutes, until golden.

6. Remove from muffin pan and top each with a tiny sliver of butter, ¼ teaspoon lemon juice, ½ teaspoon powdered sugar and one hulled, sliced strawberry.

7. Serve with maple syrup.

Dutch babies are a cross between a pancake and a crepe and bake up golden and puffy. They make a delicious change for breakfast.

CALORIES	69 calories (without syrup)
FAT	3.6 grams
PROTEIN	3 grams
SODIUM	42 mg
CARBOHYDRATES	5.5 grams
SUGARS	0.7 gram
FIBER	0.2 gram

hash brown cups

Makes 6

 Jumbo

1½ cups refrigerated shredded
  hash brown potatoes
⅛ teaspoon onion powder
Salt and pepper
3 teaspoons olive oil
6 eggs
¼ cup shredded cheddar cheese
3 slices deli ham, chopped
Optional: 6 chopped cherry
  tomatoes
Optional: 3 teaspoons chopped
  frozen spinach, defrosted and
  squeezed dry

1. Preheat oven to 400°F, and prepare 6 jumbo muffin cups by spraying well.

2. Divide the hash browns among the tins, pressing to make a nest with an indentation in the center.

3. Sprinkle onion powder and salt and pepper over the hash browns.

4. Drizzle olive oil over the hash browns.

5. Bake for 25 minutes, taking out of the oven halfway through to spray with cooking spray.

6. Crack 1 egg, and place the contents in 1 nest you made in the hash browns. Repeat for the rest of the eggs.

7. Divide the cheese and ham among the cups.

8. Add tomatoes and spinach, if using.

9. Sprinkle the tops with salt and pepper.

10. Bake for 11 minutes, until the whites of the eggs are completely set.

You can buy bags of shredded hash browns in the refrigerated section of your grocery store, near the dairy section.

CALORIES	170 calories
FAT	9.4 grams
PROTEIN	10.9 grams
SODIUM	318 mg
CARBOHYDRATES	10.3 grams
SUGARS	0.2 gram
FIBER	0.9 gram

donut bites

Makes 24

 Mini

⅓ cup butter, softened
½ cup sugar
1 egg
1 cup flour
½ teaspoon salt
½ teaspoon nutmeg
¼ cup light sour cream
¼ cup skim milk
½ cup crispy rice cereal

Topping
6 tablespoons butter
½ cup sugar
½ teaspoon cinnamon

1. Preheat oven to 350°F and prepare 24 mini muffin cups by spraying with cooking spray.

2. Mix butter and sugar, then add egg.

3. Stir in flour, salt, nutmeg, sour cream, and milk until combined.

4. Gently stir in rice cereal, then divide among muffin cups.

5. Bake for 11 minutes, until a cake tester comes out clean.

6. While they are baking, make the topping. Melt the 6 tablespoons butter in a bowl. In another bowl, mix the ½ cup sugar with the ½ teaspoon cinnamon. Set aside.

7. When ready, remove the donuts from the oven. Allow to rest 1–2 minutes. Dip in butter, then roll in cinnamon-sugar mixture. Serve immediately.

This recipe is a big favorite in my house and likely will be in yours, too. These are best served warm, fresh from the oven, but there usually aren't any leftovers.

CALORIES	109 calories
FAT	5.6 grams
PROTEIN	1 gram
SODIUM	58 mg
CARBOHYDRATES	13.2 grams
SUGARS	8.6 grams
FIBER	0.2 gram

smoky saucy stuffed eggs

Makes 6

 Regular

6 hardboiled eggs, peeled
⅛ teaspoon dry mustard
¼ teaspoon salt, divided
¼ teaspoon pepper, divided
½ teaspoon fresh chopped parsley
2 teaspoons plain low-fat or fat-free yogurt
⅛ teaspoon paprika
⅛ teaspoon smoked paprika
2 slices cooked bacon, crumbled
6 toasted baguette slices, about ½" thick and no wider in diameter than the bottom of the muffin cup
2 tablespoons butter
1 tablespoon flour
¼ cup heavy cream
¼ cup skim milk
¼ cup grated Havarti cheese

1. Preheat oven to 400°F, and prepare 6 regular muffin cups with silicone liners.

2. Cut the eggs in half and remove the yolks, placing them in a bowl. Set the whites aside.

3. Add dry mustard, ⅛ teaspoon salt, ⅛ teaspoon pepper, parsley, yogurt, both kinds of paprika, and bacon to yolks, and completely combine.

4. Stuff filling into egg whites, mounding slightly to use it all.

5. Place 1 baguette slice in each muffin cup. Place one egg half on top of each.

6. Melt butter in a small saucepan over medium heat, and stir in flour, cooking for about 1 minute.

7. Stir in ⅛ teaspoon salt, ⅛ teaspoon pepper, cream, milk, and cheese. Stir until combined and cheese is melted.

8. Spoon sauce over eggs.

9. Bake for 7–10 minutes until bubbly and hot.

Tired of the same old scrambled eggs? This is a different way to make breakfast eggs—a riff on eggs Benedict you're sure to enjoy.

CALORIES	277 calories
FAT	15.4 grams
PROTEIN	13.9 grams
SODIUM	475 mg
CARBOHYDRATES	20.7 grams
SUGARS	2.1 grams
FIBER	0.9 gram

italian breakfast biscuit

Makes 8

 Jumbo

1 tube jumbo refrigerated
   biscuits
1 cup part-skim ricotta cheese
2 teaspoons Italian seasoning
8 medium eggs
Salt and pepper, to taste

1. Preheat oven to 400°F, and prepare 8 jumbo muffin cups.

2. Place one biscuit in each cup, and press into bottom and all the way up the side.

3. Mix ricotta with Italian seasoning, and place 2 tablespoons in each cup, spreading it all around the inside.

4. Scramble each egg in a bowl then pour into a muffin cup, and season with salt and pepper.

5. Bake for 20 minutes until the egg is set.

This is a simple, delicious recipe to start the day. The protein and carbs will help you feel full and won't give you the energy crash that sweet, sugary breakfasts can.

CALORIES	205 calories
FAT	9.7 grams
PROTEIN	11.8 grams
SODIUM	439 mg
CARBOHYDRATES	16.9 grams
SUGARS	3.3 grams
FIBER	0.5 gram

Chapter 3

Beef and Pork

You may be surprised to find that there are many delicious beef and pork entrées you can make using muffin tins. I've recreated many popular dishes into muffin tin meals in this chapter. Your portion size will be controlled, and serving is easy and fun. Kids are fascinated by muffin tin entrées, so use this as a way to expand your child's diet and introduce new foods.

mexican meatloaf

Makes 6

 Regular

1 pound lean ground beef
½ cup canned kidney beans,
 drained and rinsed
3 tablespoons chopped green
 chiles from a can
¼ teaspoon salt
½ cup plus 2 tablespoons salsa
 (choose your level of heat)
6 tablespoons stone-ground
 cornmeal
2 egg whites
Pepper to taste
¼ cup grated cheddar cheese,
 plus ½ cup for topping
Light sour cream, for garnish

1. Preheat oven to 400°F.

2. Prepare 6 regular muffin cups by spraying or lining with foil or silicone cups.

3. Combine ingredients in a bowl.

4. Divide mixture among the muffin cups.

5. Top with reserved cheese.

6. Bake for 15 minutes, until cooked. Refer to the "Meat Temperature Chart" in the Introduction, for doneness.

7. Serve with sour cream on the side.

Serve these as is, or cut them in half and place inside tortillas with lettuce, tomato, and salsa, for a tasty taco treat.

CALORIES	260 calories
FAT	10.8 grams
PROTEIN	29.1 grams
SODIUM	457 mg
CARBOHYDRATES	11.6 grams
SUGARS	0.6 gram
FIBER	2.1 grams

philly cheesesteak muffins

Makes 6

 Jumbo

1 sweet onion, peeled, thinly
   sliced
1 tablespoon olive oil
2 tubes refrigerated crescent roll
   dough (8 pieces each)
12 thin slices deli roast beef
3 slices provolone cheese
Optional: Cheez Whiz, for
   serving

1. Preheat oven to 375°F.

2. Prepare 6 jumbo muffin cups.

3. Cook onion in olive oil over medium heat in a sauté pan, until the onion is golden brown and soft.

4. Open the crescent roll tubes, and unroll the dough. Each tube usually has 8 triangles. You want to push the edges together of two triangles to create a rectangle. Repeat so you have 4 rectangles. Do the same with the second tube, but only create 2 rectangles (use the rest of the dough for something else).

5. Take a rectangle of dough and place it in a jumbo muffin cup so that it is centered, with edges hanging over. Press it up the side a bit on the short sides.

6. Place 2 slices of roast beef inside each, allowing the edges to drape over on top of the dough.

7. Divide the onion among the cups.

8. Place half a piece of cheese in each, folded in half.

9. Fold the roast beef in, and then fold the dough in, pinching it in the middle and pinching it with the shorter sides as best you can.

10. Bake for 15 minutes until crescent rolls are browned and cheese has melted. Serve with Cheez Whiz, if desired.

You can now buy sheets of crescent roll dough that have not been divided into triangles. If you use a tube of this, simply cut each sheet into 4 rectangles.

CALORIES	315 calories
FAT	19.4 grams
PROTEIN	12 grams
SODIUM	548 mg
CARBOHYDRATES	23 grams
SUGARS	6.4 grams
FIBER	0.2 gram

italian sausage rice patties

Makes 6 Regular

1 cup cooked brown rice
1 mild Italian sausage link,
    removed from casing
½ cup cooked, chopped
    broccolini
1 egg
Salt and pepper
1 tablespoon shredded part-skim
    mozzarella cheese

1. Preheat oven to 400°F, and prepare 6 regular muffin cups with silicone or foil liners.

2. Mix all ingredients in a bowl, then divide among muffin cups.

3. Bake for 13 minutes until meat is cooked. Refer to the "Meat Temperature Chart" in the Introduction for doneness.

I use mild Italian sausage in this recipe, but you can use medium or hot, if you prefer. You can also substitute broccoli or other vegetables, if you prefer, for the broccolini.

CALORIES	103 calories
FAT	4.8 grams
PROTEIN	5.1 grams
SODIUM	215 mg
CARBOHYDRATES	9.3 grams
SUGARS	0.3 gram
FIBER	1 gram

sloppy joe cupcakes

Makes 12

 Regular

1 pound lean ground beef
1 medium onion, chopped
1 red bell pepper, chopped
1 garlic clove, chopped
1 tablespoon olive oil
1 15-ounce can diced Mexican
   or chili tomatoes
2 teaspoons apple cider vinegar
⅔ cup bottled chili sauce
2 teaspoons Worcestershire
   sauce
½ cup beef broth
2 sheets premade refrigerated
   pie crust

1. Preheat oven to 400°F and prepare 12 regular muffin cups.

2. In a sauté pan, cook beef, onion, red pepper, garlic, and olive oil over medium high heat, stirring to break up the meat, until browned.

3. Add tomatoes, vinegar, chili sauce, Worcestershire sauce, and beef broth and cook, stirring occasionally, until the mixture thickens, about 5 minutes.

4. Follow instructions for pie crust in "Using Pie Crusts" in the Introduction, using both crusts. Place pie crusts in cups.

5. Fill the crusts with the mixture and bake for 13 minutes. Refer to the "Meat Temperature Chart" in the Introduction, for doneness.

Sloppy Joes are still sloppy enough to please your kids with this recipe. Enjoy these mini pies with a fork.

CALORIES	249 calories
FAT	11.9 grams
PROTEIN	12.8 grams
SODIUM	468 mg
CARBOHYDRATES	23 grams
SUGARS	2.4 grams
FIBER	1.9 grams

stuffed pork tenderloin

Makes 6

Regular

1 pound pork tenderloin, trimmed
2 slices sourdough bread, torn into 1" pieces
1 clove garlic, chopped
Salt and pepper to taste
1 tablespoon chopped parsley
1 teaspoon olive oil
¼ cup chicken broth
¼ teaspoon dried thyme
¾ teaspoon balsamic vinegar
½ teaspoon garlic powder

1. Preheat oven to 400°F.

2. Prepare 6 regular muffin cups by spraying or lining with foil or silicone cups.

3. Cut the tenderloin into 6 pieces.

4. Mix bread, garlic, salt, pepper, parsley, olive oil, chicken broth, and thyme in a bowl and allow to stand until mixture is softened.

5. Take each piece of meat and butterfly it, cutting in from the side, almost to the other side, and open it like a book.

6. Place stuffing on the bottom half, and flip the top of the meat over it, closing "the book." Repeat for all pieces.

7. Place the pieces of stuffed meat in the cups (it's okay if they stick up over the top of the cups).

8. Season the meat with salt and pepper, and sprinkle ⅛ teaspoon balsamic vinegar and a pinch of garlic powder on top of each.

9. Bake for 15 minutes, then allow to rest for 3–5 minutes. Refer to the "Meat Temperature Chart" in the Introduction for doneness.

Stale bread works best for recipes like this, since it can absorb more moisture. If you don't have stale bread, just lightly toast the bread you do have. You can use any type of bread that you prefer in this dish.

CALORIES	177 calories
FAT	3.4 grams
PROTEIN	22.4 grams
SODIUM	191 mg
CARBOHYDRATES	12.3 grams
SUGARS	0.6 gram
FIBER	0.6 gram

beef stroganoff cups

Makes 12

 Regular

½ small onion, chopped
1 tablespoon olive oil
1 tablespoon unsalted butter
3 ounces mushrooms, sliced
6 ounces beef tenderloin, sliced thin
2 tablespoons Wondra flour
¾ cup beef broth
Pinch of nutmeg
Salt and pepper to taste
½ cup light sour cream, plus more for topping
4 ounces cooked egg noodles

1. Preheat oven to 400°F, and prepare 12 regular muffin cups with silicone or foil liners.

2. Cook onion with olive oil and butter in skillet over medium high until translucent.

3. Add mushrooms, turn heat to medium, and cook until cooked down.

4. Add beef and cook until cooked through.

5. Stir in flour and cook about 30 seconds, stirring.

6. Stir in beef broth and add nutmeg and salt and pepper. Cook until thickened.

7. Stir in sour cream and add noodles.

8. Divide among muffin cups and place a dollop of sour cream on top of each.

9. Bake for 8 minutes until completely hot and meat is cooked . Refer to the "Meat Temperature Chart" in the Introduction for doneness.

Beef stroganoff becomes individually portioned with this recipe. Enjoy with some green beans on the side.

CALORIES	100 calories
FAT	2.9 grams
PROTEIN	4.7 grams
SODIUM	84 mg
CARBOHYDRATES	4.8 grams
SUGARS	0.5 gram
FIBER	0.3 gram

meatballs in spaghetti nests

Makes 6

 Jumbo

2 cups cooked spaghetti, cut into
    ¼" pieces
2 eggs
Salt and pepper
1 tablespoon tomato paste
½ cup seasoned bread crumbs,
    divided
¾ cup grated Parmesan cheese,
    plus 2 tablespoons, divided
1 tablespoon olive oil
1 tablespoon cream
½ pound lean ground beef
¼ teaspoon onion powder
¼ teaspoon garlic powder
½ teaspoon Italian seasoning
1½ cups spaghetti sauce, plus
    more for serving
Pinch of sugar

1. Preheat oven to 400°F, and prepare 6 jumbo muffin cups with cooking spray or silicone liners (spray these as well).

2. Mix spaghetti, 1 of the eggs, salt and pepper, tomato paste, ¼ cup bread crumbs, ¼ cup Parmesan, olive oil, and cream.

3. Press spaghetti mixture into bottom and side of cups, going between ⅓ and ⅔ of the way to the top.

4. Bake for 12 minutes.

5. Mix beef, salt, pepper, onion powder, garlic powder, the other egg, ¼ cup bread crumbs, Italian seasoning, 1 tablespoon spaghetti sauce, sugar, and 2 tablespoons Parmesan in a bowl, then form into 6 meatballs.

6. Place 1 tablespoon spaghetti sauce into each nest, then top with meatball.

7. Place 2 tablespoons sauce on top then sprinkle remaining ½ cup Parmesan cheese among the cups.

8. Bake for about 22 minutes, until meatballs are cooked through. Refer to the "Meat Temperature Chart" in the Introduction for doneness. Serve with additional sauce and Parmesan cheese.

These cups are a great way to serve spaghetti and meatballs on a buffet because it is much easier to just grab a muffin cup than trying to negotiate serving pasta, sauce, and meatballs onto a plate. They are also just perfect for weeknight family dinners.

CALORIES	356 calories
FAT	13.3 grams
PROTEIN	24 grams
SODIUM	757 mg
CARBOHYDRATES	31.6 grams
SUGARS	7.1 grams
FIBER	3.1 grams

pork and plum

Makes 6

 Jumbo

1½ cups cooked couscous
1 pound pork tenderloin,
     trimmed and cut into 6 pieces
Salt and pepper
⅛ teaspoon onion powder
⅛ teaspoon thyme
Pinch of nutmeg
2½ black plums, pits removed,
     sliced

1. Preheat oven to 350°F, and prepare 6 jumbo muffin cups with foil or silicone liners.

2. Place ¼ cup couscous in the bottom of each cup and press it down.

3. Place 1 piece of pork in each cup and season with salt, pepper, onion powder, thyme, and nutmeg.

4. Divide plum slices among the cups, placing on top of and around the pork.

5. Bake for 40 minutes. Refer to the "Meat Temperature Chart" in the Introduction for doneness.

Plum is a perfect complement to pork in this dish, giving a nice hint of sweetness to the savory flavors. I used black plums, but other varieties would be just as good.

CALORIES	164 calories
FAT	2.4 grams
PROTEIN	21.5 grams
SODIUM	69 mg
CARBOHYDRATES	12.3 grams
SUGARS	2.8 grams
FIBER	1 gram

grown-up bologna sandwiches

Makes 6

 Jumbo

6 slices German bologna
18 slices of bread
6 tablespoons goat cheese or
    light Boursin cheese
6 tablespoons french-fried crispy
    onions (packaged)

1. Preheat oven to 400°F, and prepare 6 jumbo muffin cups by spraying with cooking spray.

2. Place 1 slice of bologna in each cup, pushing it down to conform to the cup, edges sticking up, and bake for 10 minutes until it browns (or even blackens, if you like it that way).

3. Cut out a circle from each slice of bread, roughly the size of a muffin cup (you can use the bottom of the tin or a silicone jumbo cup liner as a template).

4. Spread 1 tablespoon of cheese on each of 6 slices of bread.

5. Press the cheese-slathered pieces into the bologna cups, cheese side up (you may need to hold the edge of bologna with a fork as you maneuver the bread into the cup).

6. Return to oven for about 3–5 minutes, until the cheese melts.

7. Remove from oven, and place the contents of each cup on top of a circle of bread.

8. Sprinkle 1 tablespoon of onions on top of each sandwich, then press one more circle of bread on the top, creating a little triple-decker sandwich. Serve.

I grew up on fried bologna sandwiches and am so excited to have a reimagined way to make them in muffin tins! Use white sandwich bread if you want your sandwich to be very nostalgic, or dress it up with different types like pumpernickel, rye, or sourdough (mix it up within each sandwich even) for a very fancy sandwich. Add ketchup if you like. If you're making this for kids, use American cheese.

CALORIES	333 calories
FAT	4.8 grams
PROTEIN	10 grams
SODIUM	699 mg
CARBOHYDRATES	41.4 grams
SUGARS	4.5 grams
FIBER	1.8 grams

beef shepherd's pie

Makes 6

 Regular

Potatoes:

1½ pounds Yukon Gold potatoes
3 tablespoons unsalted butter
Salt and pepper, to taste
3 tablespoons light sour cream
2 tablespoons skim milk

Pies:

1 premade unbaked pie crust
1 tablespoon olive oil
¼ medium onion, chopped
½ pound sirloin steak, trimmed,
    sliced thinly, then cut in half
7 baby bella or white mush-
    rooms, sliced thinly
2 tablespoons Wondra flour
¾ cup beef broth
¼ teaspoon thyme
Salt and pepper to taste
1 teaspoon A1 Steak Sauce

1. Peel potatoes and cut into quarters.

2. Place in a pot of cold water and bring to a boil, boiling until they are fork tender.

3. Drain potatoes and return to pot and mash with a masher or electric mixer, adding in unsalted butter, salt, pepper, sour cream, and milk and mashing until fluffy.

Pies:

1. Preheat oven to 350°F and prepare 6 regular muffin cups.

2. Cut out 6 rounds from the pie crust, as described in "Using Pie Crusts" in the Introduction, and place in muffin cups.

3. Add oil and onion to a skillet and cook over medium heat until the onion is softened.

4. Add beef and mushrooms, cooking until beef is browned.

5. Add Wondra and stir for a minute or two.

6. Add broth, thyme, salt, pepper and steak sauce, and stir until combined.

7. Cook for about 3–4 minutes, until thickened then divide among muffin cups.

8. Top with mashed potatoes.

9. Bake for 20 minutes. Refer to the "Meat Temperature Chart" in the Introduction for doneness.

CALORIES	401 calories
FAT	20.2 grams
PROTEIN	15 grams
SODIUM	343 mg
CARBOHYDRATES	49.2 grams
SUGARS	1.6 grams
FIBER	1.9 grams

Shepherd's pie is traditionally made with ground lamb, which you can use if preferred, but I like to make it with chopped beef. With the mashed potatoes on top, this looks like a real cupcake with frosting on top (keep that in mind as something fun for April Fool's Day!).

chinese bbq pork buns

Makes 8

 Regular

½ pound chopped pork tenderloin
1 tablespoon olive oil
1 small garlic clove, chopped
Green part of 1 scallion, chopped
1 tablespoon water
1 tablespoon cornstarch
1 tablespoon tamari sauce
1 tablespoon oyster sauce
2 tablespoons hoisin sauce
1 tablespoon honey
1 tube of jumbo canned biscuits (8 pieces)

1. Preheat oven to 400°F, and prepare 8 regular muffin cups.

2. Cook pork, oil and garlic over medium high heat until pork is cooked through.

3. Stir in scallions.

4. Mix water and cornstarch, then add to pork.

5. Stir in tamari, oyster sauce, hoisin sauce, and honey.

6. On your work surface, press each biscuit until it is about 5" round.

7. Place a heaping tablespoon of pork mixture in the center of each biscuit and press the edges together at the top (so that it looks like a Hershey's Kiss), then place the biscuit in the muffin tin seam side up.

8. Bake for 12 minutes. Refer to the "Meat Temperature Chart" in the Introduction for doneness.

Cha Shao Bao are traditional Chinese steamed buns that are filled with barbecued pork, often served as part of dim sum. Oyster and hoisin sauces can be found jarred in the Asian section of your supermarket. Both sauces are very thick and rich. Oyster sauce (which does not have actual oysters in it, but oyster extract) tends to be saltier, while hoisin sauce tends to be sweeter.

CALORIES	249 calories
FAT	8.6 grams
PROTEIN	10.9 grams
SODIUM	848 mg
CARBOHYDRATES	31.6 grams
SUGARS	7.4 grams
FIBER	0.7 gram

ham and asparagus cups

Makes 4

 Regular

4 large round or oval slices deli ham
½ bunch asparagus, trimmed and cut into 1" pieces
1 teaspoon Dijon mustard
Salt and pepper to taste
1 teaspoon Wondra flour
2 tablespoons heavy cream
1 croissant, torn into 1–2" pieces
1 egg white
2 tablespoons shredded Swiss cheese

1. Preheat oven to 400°F and prepare 4 regular muffin cups by spraying with cooking spray.

2. Place ham in each cup as a liner, allowing excess to just drape over the sides.

3. Mix all other ingredients in a bowl, then divide among cups.

4. Bake for 20 minutes, until custard is set.

Ham makes the perfect container for asparagus in a creamy sauce. This dish can be a side, an entrée, or a breakfast or brunch dish.

CALORIES	155 calories
FAT	8.5 grams
PROTEIN	8.6 grams
SODIUM	451 mg
CARBOHYDRATES	9.8 grams
SUGARS	2.3 grams
FIBER	1.5 grams

taco mini pies

Makes 6

 Regular

1 refrigerated unbaked pie crust
½ pound lean ground beef
2 tablespoons canned black beans
1 plum tomato, chopped
¼ teaspoon onion powder
¼ teaspoon cumin
¼ teaspoon oregano
Salt and pepper
2 tablespoons chopped green chiles
¼ cup queso fresco cheese
1 tablespoon light sour cream
2 tablespoons salsa (heat level of your choice)
2 tablespoons shredded taco cheese
Sliced avocado, light sour cream, salsa, and/or diced tomato, for topping

1. Preheat oven to 350°F.

2. Follow instructions in "Using Pie Crusts" in the Introduction to prepare pie crust. Place in 6 cups in regular muffin tin.

3. Place the beef, beans, tomato, onion powder, cumin, oregano, salt, pepper, and chiles in a pan, and cook until beef is browned.

4. Stir in queso fresco, sour cream, and salsa.

5. Divide among muffin tins.

6. Sprinkle taco cheese on top.

7. Bake for 20 minutes. Refer to the "Meat Temperature Chart" in the Introduction for doneness.

Serve with sliced avocado, additional light sour cream, additional chopped tomato, and/or additional salsa. You can substitute ground turkey for the beef in this recipe, if you prefer.

CALORIES	279 calories
FAT	14.6 grams
PROTEIN	15.6 grams
SODIUM	383 mg
CARBOHYDRATES	20.7 grams
SUGARS	0.7 gram
FIBER	1.2 grams

spice-rubbed pork tenderloin

Makes 6

 Jumbo

1 teaspoon cinnamon
½ teaspoon cloves
½ teaspoon garlic powder
½ teaspoon salt
½ teaspoon ground pepper
½ teaspoon nutmeg
1½ cups cooked rice
1 pork tenderloin, about 1
    pound, trimmed and cut into
    6 pieces
3 teaspoons maple syrup

1. Preheat oven to 400°F and prepare 6 jumbo muffin cups with silicone or foil liners.

2. Mix spices together in a small bowl.

3. Place ¼ cup rice in each muffin cup.

4. Rub spice mix on each piece of pork and place on top of rice.

5. Drizzle maple syrup on top of pork.

6. Bake for 20 minutes. Refer to the "Meat Temperature Chart" in the Introduction for doneness.

This dish just says "fall" and feels hearty and filling. Serve with Duchess Potatoes (in Chapter 6) and Caramel Apple Mini Pies (in Chapter 9).

CALORIES	171 calories
FAT	2.5 grams
PROTEIN	20.1 grams
SODIUM	237 mg
CARBOHYDRATES	14.2 grams
SUGARS	2.1 grams
FIBER	0.6 gram

bur-ogies

Makes 6

 Jumbo

½ pound lean ground beef
1 garlic clove, chopped
Salt and pepper
¼ teaspoon dried thyme
¼ cup shredded cheddar
   cheese, plus 1 tablespoon
   reserved
¼ cup light sour cream
⅛ teaspoon dry mustard
1 tablespoon chopped fresh
   chives
6 potato pierogies, defrosted

1. Preheat oven to 400°F and prepare 6 jumbo muffin cups by spraying with cooking spray.

2. Mix meat, garlic, salt, pepper, thyme, cheddar, sour cream, mustard, and chives in a bowl.

3. Divide the meat mixture in half.

4. Divide the first half of the meat among the 6 muffin cups, pressing into the bottom.

5. Place a pierogie on top of each.

6. Divide the rest of the meat among the tins, pressing onto the pierogies.

7. Divide reserved cheddar cheese among the cups.

8. Bake 20 minutes. Refer to the "Meat Temperature Chart" in the Introduction for doneness.

My daughter came up with the name for this dish, which is a combination of pierogies (a traditional Polish dish that is dough stuffed with potatoes and folded into half-moon shapes) and ground beef. They are truly addictive.

CALORIES	167 calories
FAT	6.3 grams
PROTEIN	14.6 grams
SODIUM	269 mg
CARBOHYDRATES	12 grams
SUGARS	0.4 gram
FIBER	0.4 gram

reuben pies

Makes 6

 Regular

1 unbaked refrigerated pie crust
⅓ cup light mayonnaise
1 teaspoon ketchup
1 teaspoon lemon juice
⅛ teaspoon sugar
Pinch onion powder
½ teaspoon Worcestershire
   sauce
Pinch of celery salt
¼ pound deli corned beef,
   chopped
½ cup prepared sauerkraut
¼ cup shredded Swiss cheese,
   plus 2 tablespoons for
   topping
¼ teaspoon caraway seeds

1. Preheat oven to 400°F and prepare 6 regular muffin cups.

2. Follow the instructions in "Using Pie Crusts" in the Introduction.

3. Mix mayonnaise, ketchup, lemon juice, sugar, onion powder, Worcestershire, and celery salt in a medium bowl.

4. Add corned beef, sauerkraut, and cheese, and mix.

5. Divide among muffin cups, and sprinkle the tops with reserved Swiss cheese, then with caraway seeds.

6. Bake for 15 minutes until cheese is melted and pie crust is golden.

These pies are like delicious Reuben sandwiches in a cuter format. You can buy sauerkraut in a can, but I prefer to buy it refrigerated in a plastic bag, which you may find in the produce or meat section of your grocery store.

CALORIES	253 calories
FAT	16.9 grams
PROTEIN	6.2 grams
SODIUM	545 mg
CARBOHYDRATES	18.3 grams
SUGARS	1.2 grams
FIBER	0.3 gram

pork and fig

Makes 6

 Jumbo

1 pound pork tenderloin,
   trimmed and cut into 6 pieces
¼ cup fig preserves or fig jam
1 tablespoon tamari sauce
⅛ teaspoon fresh grated
   gingerroot
⅛ teaspoon pepper
⅛ teaspoon salt
¾ teaspoon sherry
1½ cups cooked brown rice

1. Mix all ingredients except rice in a bowl and marinate about 1–2 hours in the refrigerator.

2. Preheat oven to 400°F and prepare 6 jumbo muffin cups with silicone liners.

3. Place ¼ cup rice in each cup.

4. Place 1 piece of pork in each cup. Tuck the thinner pieces in half to match the thickness of the other pieces. Divide the marinade among the cups as well.

5. Bake for about 20–25 minutes, depending on thickness. Refer to the "Meat Temperature Chart" in the Introduction for doneness.

Use any grain you like in this dish. Barley, quinoa, or couscous all will work nicely. Fig preserves can be found from artisan producers, so check your farmers' market. If not, you can find several brands on Amazon.com.

CALORIES	201 calories
FAT	2.3 grams
PROTEIN	21.3 grams
SODIUM	263 mg
CARBOHYDRATES	20.9 grams
SUGARS	6.5 grams
FIBER	1.1 grams

cornish pasties

Makes 6

 Regular

2 premade refrigerated pie crusts
½ small onion, chopped
4 baby carrots, chopped
½ cup cooked steak, cut into ½" cubes
¼ cup refrigerated shredded hash brown potatoes
1 tablespoon skim milk
Salt and pepper
⅛ teaspoon thyme
2 tablespoons beef broth
1 egg

1. Preheat oven to 400°F and prepare 6 regular muffin cups.

2. Cut pie crust, following instructions in "Using Pie Crusts" in the Introduction, except cut the 6th piece from the second sheet of crust, then cut an additional 6 circles (lids for the cups), each about 2½" across (a 10.5-ounce can of cream soup is exactly the right size).

3. Mix all other ingredients, except egg, in a bowl, and divide among the cups.

4. Place the lids on the pies and pinch them a little along the edges to attach the lids to the sides (this does not need to be perfect).

5. Beat egg with 1 teaspoon water and brush the lids with it.

6. Bake for 15 minutes until pie crust is golden.

Cornish pasties are traditionally half-moon shaped pastries stuffed with meat, potato, and vegetables. This version simplifies the process by using premade pie crusts and baking in muffin cups.

CALORIES	317 calories
FAT	18.6 grams
PROTEIN	5.2 grams
SODIUM	416 mg
CARBOHYDRATES	34.9 grams
SUGARS	0.7 gram
FIBER	0.4 gram

gyro meatloaf

Makes 12

 Regular

½ pound lean hamburger
½ pound ground lamb
3 teaspoons oregano
¼ teaspoon pepper
¼ teaspoon onion powder
2 cloves garlic, minced
½ cup seasoned bread crumbs
2 eggs
2 teaspoons chopped fresh
    parsley
2 tablespoons chopped sundried
    tomatoes
½ cup feta cheese

Topping
1 cup plain Greek low-fat or fat-
    free yogurt
¼ teaspoon oregano
¼ teaspoon pepper
¼ cup feta cheese

1. Preheat oven to 400°F, and prepare 12 regular muffin cups by spraying with cooking spray.

2. Mix all ingredients except items reserved for topping.

3. Divide among muffin cups.

4. To make topping, mix yogurt, oregano, pepper, and feta, and spread on the top of the cups.

5. Bake for about 15 minutes, until cooked through. Refer to the "Meat Temperature Chart" in the Introduction for doneness.

Enjoy these as is, or break them apart and eat in a pita with Greek salad.

CALORIES	171 calories
FAT	8.9 grams
PROTEIN	14.7 grams
SODIUM	257 mg
CARBOHYDRATES	5.2 grams
SUGARS	1.7 grams
FIBER	0.4 gram

corndog cups

Makes 8

 Regular

1 cup plus 2 tablespoons
   cornmeal
¼ cup plus 1 tablespoon flour
⅛ teaspoon salt
¼ cup vegetable oil
½ cup skim milk
Pinch of pepper
Pinch of dry mustard
¼ teaspoon baking powder
1 tablespoon sugar
3 hot dogs, roughly chopped
1 tablespoon ketchup
1 tablespoon yellow mustard
1 teaspoon Worcestershire sauce
½ teaspoon brown sugar

1. Preheat oven to 400°F and prepare 8 regular muffin cups by spraying with cooking spray.

2. Mix cornmeal, flour, salt, vegetable oil, milk, pepper, dry mustard, baking powder, and sugar together in a bowl.

3. Divide among muffin cups and press into the bottom and up the sides of the cups.

4. Bake 10–13 minutes until crust is set (bake longer if you want your crust to be super crunchy or a bit less if you would like it a tad softer).

5. Mix hot dogs, ketchup, mustard, Worcestershire, and brown sugar in a bowl, then divide among cups.

6. Bake for 10 minutes until hot dogs are hot.

This is a kid favorite and actually easier to eat than a traditional corn dog on a stick.

CALORIES	212 calories
FAT	12.2 grams
PROTEIN	4.4 grams
SODIUM	288 mg
CARBOHYDRATES	20.7 grams
SUGARS	3.5 grams
FIBER	1.4 grams

stuffed cube steak

Makes 4

 Jumbo

4 cube steaks
8 white or baby bella
   mushrooms
6 baby carrots
¼ of a red bell pepper
3 ounces zucchini (about ½ of a
   small one)
½ cup seasoned bread crumbs
Salt and pepper
1 small shallot
1 clove garlic
8 cherry tomatoes

1. Preheat oven to 400°F and prepare 4 jumbo muffin cups by spraying with cooking spray.

2. Place 1 cube steak in each cup, pushing it down in the center to fill the cup (the edges will stick up). Season with salt and pepper.

3. Place all other ingredients in a food processor and chop finely.

4. Divide stuffing among cups, then bake for 20 minutes, until beef is completely cooked. Refer to the "Meat Temperature Chart" in the Introduction for doneness.

The cube steak itself forms the cup in this dish. You could also add some hash browns to the vegetable mix. This is delicious by itself but could also be served with beef gravy.

CALORIES	284 calories
FAT	4.4 grams
PROTEIN	45.1 grams
SODIUM	355 mg
CARBOHYDRATES	15.9 grams
SUGARS	4.1 grams
FIBER	2.4 grams

cheeseburger pies

Makes 6

 Regular

1 refrigerated unbaked pie crust
1 tablespoon chopped onion
10 ounces ground beef
2 tablespoons ketchup
1 tablespoon yellow mustard
1 tablespoon relish
2 tablespoons seasoned bread
   crumbs
Salt and pepper to taste
¼ cup shredded cheddar cheese
1½ slices American cheese
Ketchup, mustard, and relish, for
   serving

1. Preheat oven to 400°F and prepare 6 regular muffin cups.

2. Prepare pie crust according to instructions in "Using Pie Crust" in Introduction.

3. Mix all ingredients except American cheese in a bowl until combined, then divide among cups.

4. Break the American cheese into squares by folding the full piece in half then in half again to make 4 squares, then folding the ½ piece in half once to make 2 squares, for a total of 6 squares. Place 1 square on top of each burger.

5. Bake for 20 minutes, until beef is cooked through. Refer to the "Meat Temperature Chart" in the Introduction for doneness.

Serve with additional ketchup, mustard, and relish. Sweet potato fries are a great accompaniment, as is a milkshake or smoothie if you're looking for a treat.

CALORIES	274 calories
FAT	13.7 grams
PROTEIN	17.1 grams
SODIUM	493 mg
CARBOHYDRATES	20.5 grams
SUGARS	1.8 grams
FIBER	0.3 gram

Chapter 4

Chicken and Turkey

Looking for some new and different ways to make chicken and turkey? This chapter shows you how muffin tins can make cooking poultry new and fresh. Whether you're looking for something quick and simple, or a dish that's more complex, you'll find them all in this chapter. These individually sized dishes are pretty and fun to serve.

cornmeal-crusted mustard chicken with sweet potato coins 🌱

Makes 4

Regular

1 yam or sweet potato, peeled and sliced into ¼" coins
1 tablespoon honey
1 tablespoon olive oil
Salt and pepper, to taste
2 boneless skinless chicken breasts
2 egg whites
2 tablespoons Dijon mustard
2 tablespoons water
½ cup cornmeal
½ teaspoon dried rosemary

1. Preheat oven to 350°F.

2. Place 4 muffin liners in a regular muffin tin.

3. Place 1 yam coin at the bottom of each.

4. Mix honey and olive oil and brush each coin with the mixture.

5. Season with salt and pepper.

6. Cut the chicken breasts into 4 pieces of equal size, about the width of a muffin cup.

7. Mix egg white, mustard, and water in a small bowl.

8. On a small plate, mix cornmeal, rosemary, and salt and pepper.

9. Dip each piece of chicken in the egg mixture, then dredge it in the cornmeal mixture.

10. Place one piece of chicken on top of each yam coin.

11. Spray the chicken with cooking spray.

12. Bake for 13 minutes, then using tongs, flip each piece of chicken over, and spray the top with cooking spray.

13. Return to the oven and bake for another 13 minutes, then broil for 3 minutes. Refer to the "Meat Temperature Chart" in the Introduction for doneness.

The crunchy chicken provides a nice contrast to the soft yam in this dish. Enjoy with Lucky Bamboo Asparagus (see Chapter 7).

CALORIES	201 calories
FAT	4.8 grams
PROTEIN	15.9 grams
SODIUM	174 mg
CARBOHYDRATES	23.1 grams
SUGARS	5.6 grams
FIBER	2.4 grams

turkey tetrazzini

Makes 6

 Jumbo

2 cups cooked spaghetti
1 tablespoon olive oil
Salt and pepper
½ small onion, chopped
1 tablespoon butter
5 button mushrooms, thinly sliced
2 tablespoons Wondra flour
½ cup chicken broth
½ cup skim milk
Pinch nutmeg
1 tablespoon lemon juice
1 tablespoon chopped parsley
1 tablespoon sherry
18 thin turkey tenderloin slices
     (each about 4" long)
6 teaspoons grated Swiss cheese
6 teaspoons grated Parmesan
     cheese

1. Preheat oven to 400°F and prepare 6 cups in a jumbo muffin tin with foil or silicone liners.

2. Toss spaghetti with olive oil and salt and pepper and divide among cups, making nests in the cups.

3. Cook onion and butter over medium heat in a skillet, until onion is translucent.

4. Add in mushrooms, and cook until they cook down and are soft.

5. Stir in Wondra and cook 1 minute.

6. Add chicken broth and milk, cooking until thickened.

7. Add ½ teaspoon salt, nutmeg, lemon juice, parsley, and sherry and cook for another minute or two.

8. Place 1 tablespoon sauce over each pasta nest, then top with 3 turkey tenderloins.

9. Divide remaining sauce over the tops of the turkey, letting some run down under the turkey.

10. Sprinkle cheeses on top.

11. Bake about 20 minutes until turkey is cooked through. Refer to the "Meat Temperature Chart" in the Introduction for doneness.

An easy change to this recipe is to use refrigerated linguine cups instead of cooked pasta. If you do so, first plunge them into boiling water for about 3 minutes to get them partially cooked.

CALORIES	225 calories
FAT	7.3 grams
PROTEIN	18.3 grams
SODIUM	132 mg
CARBOHYDRATES	19 grams
SUGARS	2 grams
FIBER	1.3 grams

apricot-lime chicken

Makes 6

 Jumbo

3 boneless, skinless chicken breasts
2 tablespoons tamari sauce (or soy sauce)
2 tablespoons lime juice
½ cup apricot preserves
Pepper to taste
½ teaspoon dried cilantro, or 1 teaspoon fresh, chopped, plus additional for garnish

1. Preheat oven to 350°F.

2. Spray a 6-cup jumbo muffin tin (or line with silicone or foil cups).

3. Cut the chicken breasts in half, holding your knife parallel to the cutting board so they are the same length, but half the thickness.

4. Place the chicken and remaining ingredients in a zip-top bag, and marinate in the refrigerator for 20 minutes to 2 hours.

5. Place one piece of marinated chicken in each cup, forming a "U" so it fits inside the cup.

6. Garnish with cilantro.

7. Bake for 30 minutes. Refer to the "Meat Temperature Chart" in the Introduction for doneness.

Apricot and lime might not be flavors you've tried together before, but they work extremely well together, giving a balance of sweet and sour.

CALORIES	129 calories
FAT	0.8 gram
PROTEIN	12.9 grams
SODIUM	345 mg
CARBOHYDRATES	17.9 grams
SUGARS	11.8 grams
FIBER	0.2 gram

chicken florentine meatloaf

Makes 6

 Regular

1 pound lean ground chicken

1 clove garlic, chopped

Salt and pepper, to taste

1 egg

½ teaspoon dried bouquet garni herb mix (substitute a mix of dried thyme, rosemary, and parsley, if you can't find this)

¾ of a 10-ounce box of frozen chopped spinach, defrosted and squeezed dry

¼ cup seasoned bread crumbs

¼ cup shredded fontina cheese, plus an additional ¼ cup for topping, if desired

3 baby bella or white mushrooms, chopped

⅛ teaspoon onion powder

¼ cup tomato sauce

3 cherry tomatoes, halved, if desired for topping

1. Preheat oven to 350°F.

2. Prepare a regular 6-cup muffin tin by spraying or lining with foil or silicone liners.

3. Mix all ingredients except cherry tomatoes in a bowl.

4. Divide among muffin cups.

5. Top with cheese and/or half a cherry tomato on each.

6. Bake for 20 minutes. Refer to the "Meat Temperature Chart" in the Introduction for doneness.

These yummy Italian chicken meatloaves are light and flavorful. Enjoy with rice sprinkled with Parmesan.

CALORIES	209 calories
FAT	10 grams
PROTEIN	22.4 grams
SODIUM	384 mg
CARBOHYDRATES	6.6 grams
SUGARS	1.4 grams
FIBER	1.9 grams

teriyaki turkey cups

Makes 6

 Jumbo

12 turkey cutlets
¼ cup teriyaki sauce
6 round Asian rice paper wraps
3 cups chopped Napa cabbage
2 teaspoons sesame oil
Salt and pepper

1. In a nonmetal bowl, mix the turkey and teriyaki and allow to marinate for at least ½ hour (and up to 2 hours) in the refrigerator.

2. Preheat oven to 400°F and prepare 6 jumbo muffin cups with silicone liners.

3. Soak rice paper wraps in warm water until pliable.

4. Place 1 rice paper wrap in each cup, pressing down to conform to the shape of the cup.

5. Mix cabbage, sesame oil, and salt and pepper and divide among cups.

6. Place 2 turkey cutlets in each cup, folding the turkey in half to make it fit. Place marinade on top.

7. Bake for 13–18 minutes, depending on the thickness of the turkey. Refer to the "Meat Temperature Chart" in the Introduction for doneness.

The rice paper wrappers are a light and fun alternative to heavier crusts and get nice and crunchy around the edges.

CALORIES	188 calories
FAT	2.1 grams
PROTEIN	30.1 grams
SODIUM	592 mg
CARBOHYDRATES	12 grams
SUGARS	3.1 grams
FIBER	1.2 grams

moroccan chicken potpie

Makes 6

 Regular

¼ cup chopped onion
¼ cup chopped carrot
1 tablespoon olive oil
1 clove garlic, chopped
¼ cup diced red bell pepper
1 boneless, skinless chicken breast, chopped into bite-size pieces
12 dried pitted prunes, quartered
¼ cup low-sodium chicken stock
Salt and pepper, to taste
¼ cup pine nuts
½ teaspoon honey
⅛ teaspoon cumin
1 refrigerated unbaked pie crust
1 egg white

1. Preheat oven to 350°F, and prepare 6 regular muffin cups.

2. Add onion, carrot, and olive oil to a sauté pan, and cook over medium heat, until softened.

3. Add garlic, bell pepper, chicken, prunes, chicken stock, salt, pepper, pine nuts, honey, and cumin. Cook, stirring occasionally over medium heat, until chicken is cooked and liquid begins to thicken.

4. Allow this to rest while you prepare pie crust.

5. Follow the instructions in "Using Pie Crusts" in the Introduction to prepare the pie crust, reserving the scraps of crust. Place in muffin tin cups.

6. Place ¼ cup of the chicken mixture into each cup.

7. Lay pieces of the pie crust scraps on top, mostly covering the tops of the cups.

8. Brush with egg wash (1 egg white mixed with 2 teaspoons water).

9. Bake for 15 minutes. Refer to the "Meat Temperature Chart" in the Introduction for doneness.

The pitted prunes are the secret to this dish, adding sweetness and a depth of flavor. I like to serve this with couscous and steamed carrots.

CALORIES	266 calories
FAT	13.8 grams
PROTEIN	6.2 grams
SODIUM	224 mg
CARBOHYDRATES	31.1 grams
SUGARS	8.8 grams
FIBER	2 grams

chicken with rosemary goat cheese

Makes 6

 Jumbo

3 boneless, skinless chicken breasts, each cut in half the short way

4 ounces goat cheese

1 small shallot

¼ teaspoon salt, plus additional

⅛ teaspoon pepper, plus additional

2 tablespoons seasoned bread crumbs

2 tablespoons packed fresh rosemary leaves

1. Preheat oven to 400°F.

2. Prepare 6 jumbo muffin cups by spraying with cooking spray.

3. Make a slice along the cut side of each half chicken breast, creating a deep pocket inside it, without cutting through the other 3 sides.

4. Place goat cheese, shallot, salt, pepper, bread crumbs, and rosemary in a food processor and mix completely.

5. Stuff filling in each chicken piece, reserving what does not fit for toppings. Place in a muffin cup.

6. Divide remaining filling and place as dollops on the tops of the chicken.

7. Season with salt and pepper.

8. Bake for about 25 minutes (depending on thickness), until chicken is cooked through. Refer to the "Meat Temperature Chart" in the Introduction for doneness.

Try this dish with ricotta and Italian seasoning instead of goat cheese and rosemary. Or use any of your favorite soft cheeses and experiment with different herbs.

CALORIES	139 calories
FAT	6.2 grams
PROTEIN	16.5 grams
SODIUM	238 mg
CARBOHYDRATES	2.5 grams
SUGARS	0.6 gram
FIBER	0.1 gram

chicken parmesan in a cup

Makes 6

 Jumbo

1¼ cups spaghetti sauce
4 ounces spaghetti, cooked, ½ cup reserved
6 teaspoons grated Parmesan cheese, plus additional for garnish
¼ cup seasoned bread crumbs
2 boneless, skinless chicken breasts, cut into thirds
Salt and pepper
6 tablespoons shredded part-skim mozzarella cheese

1. Preheat the oven to 400°F, and prepare 6 jumbo muffin cups with silicone or foil liners.

2. Place 1 tablespoon spaghetti sauce in each cup.

3. Divide spaghetti among the cups.

4. Top the spaghetti with 1 tablespoon sauce and 1 teaspoon Parmesan cheese per cup.

5. Place the bread crumbs on a plate, and press one side of each piece of chicken into them. Then place the chicken, bread crumbs up, in each cup, seasoning with salt and pepper.

6. Spray the chicken lightly with cooking spray, and bake for 17 minutes. Remove from the oven, and divide the reserved spaghetti among the cups and top with 1 table-spoon sauce per cup.

7. Sprinkle mozzarella cheese on top and return to oven for 5 minutes, until cheese is melted.

8. Serve with additional Parmesan cheese.

Serving chicken Parmesan in muffin tins makes cleanup fast and easy—no more baked-on cheese to scrub from a casserole dish. These individual chicken Parmesan cups taste great with garlic bread.

CALORIES	162 calories
FAT	3.7 grams
PROTEIN	13.1 grams
SODIUM	398 mg
CARBOHYDRATES	17 grams
SUGARS	5.2 grams
FIBER	2 grams

chicken tortilla pies

Makes 6

 Jumbo

3 whole wheat tortillas

2 tablespoons chopped green chiles (from a can)

1 boneless, skinless chicken breast, cooked and chopped (about 1 cup), divided

¾ cup salsa (choose your own heat level)

½ cup light sour cream, plus 2 tablespoons for topping

¾ cup shredded Monterey Jack cheese, plus 6 tablespoons for topping

Optional: Sour cream and avocado, for serving

1. Preheat oven to 400°F and prepare 6 jumbo muffin cups with silicone liners by spraying with cooking spray.

2. Stack the 3 tortillas and using the bottom of a silicone jumbo muffin cup liner as a template, cut out 6 circles (making 18 all together).

3. Layer the cups by placing 1 tortilla circle at the bottom of each cup.

4. Place ½ teaspoon chiles in each cup.

5. Use half the chicken and divide it among the cups.

6. Place 1 tablespoon salsa in each cup.

7. Place 2 teaspoons sour cream in each cup.

8. Place 1 tablespoon cheese in each cup.

9. Repeat the layering steps, beginning with a tortilla circle.

10. Top with third tortilla circle and place 1 teaspoon sour cream and 1 tablespoon cheese on top of each.

11. Bake for 15 minutes, until cheese has melted and cups are slightly browned. Refer to the "Meat Temperature Chart" in the Introduction for doneness. Serve with additional sour cream and some avocado, if you like.

Chicken tortilla pie is delicious, but is usually hard to cut and serve. That isn't a problem when you make it in individual muffin cups.

CALORIES	142 calories
FAT	10 grams
PROTEIN	12.5 grams
SODIUM	430 mg
CARBOHYDRATES	17 grams
SUGARS	1.2 grams
FIBER	2 grams

italian chicken

Makes 4

 Jumbo

¼ cup whole pitted black olives

2 tablespoons capers with juice

4 sundried tomatoes in oil, drained

2 ounces anchovy fillets, drained

1 tablespoon lemon juice

1 tablespoon packed chopped fresh basil

1 tablespoon olive oil

Salt and pepper, to taste

½ cup orzo, cooked

⅓ cup part-skim ricotta cheese

2 boneless, skinless chicken breasts, halved the short way

1. Preheat oven to 400°F and prepare 4 jumbo muffin cups with silicone liners.

2. Place olives, capers, tomatoes, anchovies, lemon juice, basil, olive oil, and salt and pepper in food processor and process into a paste.

3. Mix orzo with ricotta and season with salt and pepper.

4. Divide orzo mixture among cups and place a chicken breast half on top.

5. Pour olive paste on top of chicken and bake for 30 minutes, until chicken is cooked through. Refer to the "Meat Temperature Chart" in the Introduction for doneness.

Orzo, also called risoni, is a small pasta that looks very much like rice. It's a fun addition to this dish, but you can also substitute the same amount of rice.

CALORIES	194 calories
FAT	8.4 grams
PROTEIN	21.4 grams
SODIUM	778 mg
CARBOHYDRATES	18.3 grams
SUGARS	0.9 gram
FIBER	1.3 grams

turkey kimchi bites

Makes 18

 Mini

½ pound lean ground turkey
⅓ cup panko
½ cup prepared kimchi
1 egg
1 tablespoon tamari sauce

1. Preheat oven to 400°F and prepare 18 mini muffin cups by spraying with cooking spray.

2. Place all ingredients in a food processor, and process until it looks like meatloaf.

3. Divide among cups and bake for 10 minutes. Refer to the "Meat Temperature Chart" in the Introduction for doneness.

4. Serve with rice and stir-fried vegetables.

Kimchi is a Korean fermented cabbage dish. You can buy it premade and bottled in Asian markets or the Asian section of your grocery store.

CALORIES	29 calories
FAT	0.5 gram
PROTEIN	4.6 grams
SODIUM	108 mg
CARBOHYDRATES	0.6 gram
SUGARS	0.1 gram
FIBER	0.1 gram

chicken paprikash

Makes 4

 Jumbo

½ small onion, chopped
1 tablespoon olive oil
1 small garlic clove, chopped
1 teaspoon Wondra flour
½ of a 14.5-ounce can of diced tomatoes
1 boneless, skinless chicken breast, cut into ½–1" pieces
1½ cups egg noodles, cooked according to package instructions
⅔ cup light sour cream, plus more for topping
Salt and pepper to taste
1 teaspoon paprika, plus more for topping

1. Preheat oven to 400°F and prepare 4 jumbo muffin cups with silicone liners.

2. Cook onion in oil over medium heat in a skillet until translucent. Add garlic and cook for 1 minute.

3. Stir in Wondra and cook for 1 minute.

4. Add tomatoes and cook until thickened. Turn off heat.

5. Stir in chicken, noodles, sour cream, salt, pepper, and paprika and combine completely.

6. Divide among cups and top each with a dollop of sour cream and a sprinkle of paprika. Bake for about 20–24 minutes until chicken is cooked through. Refer to the "Meat Temperature Chart" in the Introduction for doneness.

This traditional Hungarian dish is more manageable in individual muffin cups. Use whole wheat egg noodles if you want to up your fiber intake.

CALORIES	218 calories
FAT	8.6 grams
PROTEIN	11.1 grams
SODIUM	134 mg
CARBOHYDRATES	23.1 grams
SUGARS	0.7 gram
FIBER	1.9 grams

buffalo chicken bites

Makes 33

 Mini

1 stalk celery, chopped finely
1 pound lean ground chicken
3 tablespoons melted unsalted
    butter
Salt and pepper to taste
¾ cup panko, plus additional for
    topping
1 egg
2 tablespoons blue cheese
2 tablespoons Frank's Hot Sauce
About 6 ounces blue cheese
    dressing

1. Preheat oven to 400°F and prepare 33 mini muffin cups by spraying with cooking spray.

2. Mix all ingredients except blue cheese dressing in a bowl.

3. Divide among muffin tins, filling ¾ full.

4. Place about 1 teaspoon blue cheese dressing on top of each then sprinkle about ½ teaspoon panko on each. Spray tops with cooking spray.

5. Bake for 10 minutes until chicken is cooked through. Refer to the "Meat Temperature Chart" in the Introduction for doneness.

Panko is Japanese-style bread crumbs that cook up crisper than regular varieties. Look for it near bread crumbs or in the Asian section of your supermarket.

CALORIES	69 calories
FAT	5.2 grams
PROTEIN	3.7 grams
SODIUM	88 mg
CARBOHYDRATES	0.7 gram
SUGARS	0.2 gram
FIBER	0.1 gram

turkey cranberry cups

Makes 8

 Regular

1 tablespoon soy sauce
Pepper to taste
¼ cup prepared cranberry sauce
⅛ teaspoon onion powder
1 teaspoon Worcestershire sauce
8 turkey cutlets
1 tube refrigerated crescent roll
   dough (8 pieces)

1. Make marinade by mixing all ingredients except turkey and crescent roll dough in a bowl, until combined.

2. Place turkey in bowl and marinate for at least ½ hour and up to 2 hours in the refrigerator.

3. Preheat oven to 400°F and prepare 8 regular muffin cups.

4. Follow the instructions in "Crescent Roll Crusts" in the Introduction for crescent roll dough.

5. Place 1 turkey cutlet in each cup, tucking it around to fit.

6. Bake for 12–15 minutes, depending on the thickness of the turkey. Refer to the "Meat Temperature Chart" in the Introduction for doneness.

Enjoy this when you have a craving for Thanksgiving flavors without all the work of roasting a whole turkey. Serve with Brussels Sprouts Cups (see Chapter 7).

CALORIES	144 calories
FAT	6.1 grams
PROTEIN	9.1 grams
SODIUM	367 mg
CARBOHYDRATES	14.7 grams
SUGARS	6.4 grams
FIBER	0.1 gram

tangy nut-crusted chicken

Makes 6

 Jumbo

1 tablespoon Dijon mustard
3 tablespoons buttermilk
Salt and pepper
2 boneless, skinless chicken
   breasts, cut into thirds the
   short way
1½ cups cooked couscous
1 cup chopped pecans
6 teaspoons crumbled blue
   cheese

1. Mix mustard, buttermilk, salt and pepper in a bowl and place chicken in, turning to coat. Marinate 20 minutes to 2 hours in the refrigerator.

2. Preheat oven to 350°F and prepare 6 jumbo muffin cups with foil or silicone liners.

3. Place ¼ cup couscous in the bottom of each cup, pressing gently into the bottom and seasoning with salt and pepper.

4. Spread pecans on a plate or on waxed paper on your work surface. Remove chicken from buttermilk mixture, reserving the marinade, and press chicken pieces into pecans, coating them.

5. Place chicken on top of couscous in the cups.

6. Drizzle marinade around the chicken, onto the couscous.

7. Crumble blue cheese on top of chicken.

8. Bake for 32–37 minutes, until chicken is done. Refer to the "Meat Temperature Chart" in the Introduction for doneness.

Nuts make the chicken very crunchy, while mustard gives it a nice tang. You can substitute almonds for pecans if you prefer in this recipe.

CALORIES	225 calories
FAT	14 grams
PROTEIN	12.2 grams
SODIUM	101 mg
CARBOHYDRATES	12.2 grams
SUGARS	1.2 grams
FIBER	2.4 grams

chicken with caper and dill sauce

Makes 9

 Regular

3 boneless, skinless chicken
    breasts, cut into thirds
¾ cup light sour cream
1½ tablespoons lemon juice
1½ tablespoons capers
¾ teaspoon fresh chopped dill
    weed, plus sprigs for garnish
Salt and pepper

1. Preheat oven to 400°F and prepare 9 regular muffin cups with silicone or foil liners.

2. Mix all ingredients in a bowl, coating the chicken entirely.

3. Place 1 piece of chicken in each cup and evenly divide sauce among cups.

4. Place a small sprig of fresh dill on top of each and bake for about 14 minutes (depending on thickness of chicken). Refer to the "Meat Temperature Chart" in the Introduction for doneness.

Capers are the pickled buds of the caper bush and pack lots of flavor. You can find them near the olives or in the Italian section of your grocery store.

CALORIES	67 calories
FAT	2.5 grams
PROTEIN	8.7 grams
SODIUM	65 mg
CARBOHYDRATES	1.7 grams
SUGARS	0.1 gram
FIBER	0.1 gram

turkey goulash

Makes 7 or 8

1 cup dry elbow macaroni
¾ small onion, chopped
1 tablespoon olive oil
2 garlic cloves, chopped
½ pound lean ground turkey
2 tablespoons Wondra flour
Salt and pepper
1½ cans stewed tomatoes, with
   juice (14.5 ounce cans)
¼ teaspoon paprika
¼ teaspoon smoked paprika
   (optional, see sidebar)
½ teaspoon caraway seeds
¼ cup beef broth
¼ cup plus 2 tablespoons light
   sour cream

1. Preheat oven to 400°F, and prepare 7 or 8 jumbo muffin cups with foil or silicone liners (with liners you'll fill about 8; without liners, about 7).

2. Cook macaroni according to package directions, until al dente. Set aside.

3. Cook onion in olive oil in skillet over medium high heat until translucent, then add garlic and cook for 1 minute.

4. Stir in turkey and cook until cooked through.

5. Stir in Wondra and cook 1 minute. Add the salt and pepper.

6. Add tomatoes and juice, stirring and breaking up the tomatoes as they cook.

7. Add paprika (one or both) and caraway seeds.

8. Add beef broth and cook until mixture thickens.

9. Turn off heat and add sour cream and macaroni.

10. Divide among cups and bake for 15 minutes. Refer to the "Meat Temperature Chart" in the Introduction for doneness.

This goulash comes in convenient individual servings. Best of all, you won't have to scrub baked-on dishes afterwards! Add a little smoked paprika to kick up the flavor, if you like.

CALORIES	135 calories (assuming recipe makes 8 servings)
FAT	3.7 grams
PROTEIN	12.1 grams
SODIUM	173 mg
CARBOHYDRATES	14.1 grams
SUGARS	0.4 gram
FIBER	2 grams

individual chicken casseroles

Makes 6

 Jumbo

1 tablespoon olive oil
½ small onion, chopped
1 clove garlic, chopped
1 boneless, skinless chicken
    breast, cut into ½" pieces
2 tablespoons white wine
2 tablespoons Wondra flour
½ cup chicken broth
1 cup heavy cream
½ teaspoon dried rosemary
Salt and pepper, to taste
½ cup frozen chopped spinach,
    defrosted, and squeezed dry
4 slices whole wheat sandwich
    bread, torn into 1" pieces
Pinch nutmeg

1. Preheat oven to 400°F and prepare 6 jumbo muffin cups with foil or silicone liners.

2. Heat olive oil in a skillet over medium high heat, then add onion, stirring occasionally until translucent.

3. Add garlic and chicken, stirring occasionally until chicken is almost completely cooked.

4. Add wine and cook until it evaporates.

5. Stir in flour then cook for about 30 seconds, stirring.

6. Stir in broth, cream, rosemary and salt and pepper, and bring to a boil.

7. Turn off the heat and stir in spinach, bread, and nutmeg until combined.

8. Divide among muffin cups and bake for 15 minutes until golden and completely hot. Refer to the "Meat Temperature Chart" in the Introduction for doneness.

This is comfort food at its best and is perfect for a Sunday supper along with Squash Casserole (in Chapter 7).

CALORIES	244 calories
FAT	17 grams
PROTEIN	8.4 grams
SODIUM	208 mg
CARBOHYDRATES	12.4 grams
SUGARS	1.5 grams
FIBER	2.1 grams

mango tandoori chicken

Makes 9

 Jumbo

1 garlic clove, chopped
¼ cup chopped cilantro
1 teaspoon cumin
½ teaspoon paprika
½ teaspoon salt
¼ teaspoon ground pepper
2 tablespoons olive oil
1 tablespoon lemon juice
½ cup plain low-fat or fat-free
  yogurt
3 boneless, skinless chicken
  breasts, cut into thirds
2 cups cooked brown rice
½ cup chopped mango
2 tablespoons mango juice
Salt and pepper

1. Mix garlic, cilantro, cumin, paprika, salt, pepper, olive oil, lemon juice and yogurt in a bowl and place chicken in.

2. Cover and marinate for 1–4 hours in the refrigerator.

3. Preheat oven to 375°F and prepare 9 jumbo muffin cups with foil or silicone liners.

4. Mix rice, mango, juice, and salt and pepper and divide among cups.

5. Place 1 piece of chicken in each cup, spooning a table-spoon of marinade into the cup with it.

6. Bake for 30 minutes. Refer to the "Meat Temperature Chart" in the Introduction for doneness.

Traditional Indian tandoori chicken is cooked in a tandoor, a clay oven that is shaped like a graduated cylinder, which keeps the moisture and flavors in. Here, cooking in muffin cups helps accomplish the same thing. Mango rice makes this dish extra special.

CALORIES	130 calories
FAT	4 grams
PROTEIN	9.8 grams
SODIUM	155 mg
CARBOHYDRATES	13.1 grams
SUGARS	2.6 grams
FIBER	1 gram

sour cream and onion chicken nuggets

Makes 24

Makes 24

 Mini

1 10-ounce bag sour-cream-and-onion potato chips
2 tablespoons chopped fresh chives
½ cup light sour cream
¼ teaspoon onion powder
⅓ cup buttermilk
⅛ teaspoon ground pepper
⅛ teaspoon paprika
3 boneless, skinless chicken breasts, cut into 8 pieces each

1. Preheat oven to 375°F and prepare 24 mini muffin cups by spraying heavily with cooking spray.

2. Pulverize potato chips in a food processor and add chives, mixing thoroughly.

3. Pour onto a plate or waxed paper.

4. Mix sour cream, onion powder, buttermilk, pepper, and paprika in a bowl.

5. Dunk chicken in sour cream mixture (shaking off slightly so it is not heavily coated) and then into potato chip mixture, completely covering with coating.

6. Place 1 piece of coated chicken in each muffin cup, lightly pressing the piece into the cups (it's okay if the edge hangs out a bit).

7. Spray the tops of the chicken with cooking spray.

8. Bake 15 minutes, then broil for 2–3 minutes until brown and crispy. Refer to the "Meat Temperature Chart" in the Introduction for doneness.

This special treat will make you a hero for sure when everyone samples the spot-on sour cream and onion flavor.

CALORIES	88 calories
FAT	4.9 grams
PROTEIN	4.1 grams
SODIUM	91 mg
CARBOHYDRATES	6.6 grams
SUGARS	0.2 gram
FIBER	0.2 gram

turkey empanadas

Makes 6

 Regular

2 tablespoons raisins
1 tablespoon hot water
1 unbaked refrigerated pie crust
¼ small onion, chopped
1 teaspoon olive oil
¼ pound lean ground turkey
1 small garlic clove, chopped
1 tablespoon Wondra flour
¾ cup beef broth
4 olives, chopped
1 hardboiled egg, chopped
¼ cup refrigerated hash
    brown potatoes (chunks, not
    shredded)
Salt and pepper

1. Preheat oven to 400°F and prepare 6 regular muffin cups.

2. Place the raisins and water in a small bowl and allow to soak while you prepare other ingredients.

3. Prepare pie crust according to instructions in "Using Pie Crusts" in the Introduction.

4. Cook onion in oil over medium high until translucent.

5. Add turkey and garlic and cook until turkey is cooked through.

6. Stir in flour and cook for 1 minute.

7. Stir in broth and stir until thickened.

8. Remove from heat and stir in raisins (and remaining water), olives, egg, and potato and season with salt and pepper.

9. Divide mixture among muffin cups.

10. Bake for 15 minutes. Refer to the "Meat Temperature Chart" in the Introduction for doneness.

An empanada is a traditional South American stuffed pastry. This version reimagines it as a mini pie but is still packed with the ingredients that make it stand out.

CALORIES	207 calories
FAT	9.6 grams
PROTEIN	8.5 grams
SODIUM	354 mg
CARBOHYDRATES	21.6 grams
SUGARS	2 grams
FIBER	0.4 gram

chicken cordon bleu

Makes 4

 Regular

4 round or oval deli ham slices
1 boneless, skinless chicken
    breast, cut into ½–1" pieces
⅓ cup grated Gruyère cheese
Salt and pepper
1 tablespoon Dijon mustard
1 tablespoon chopped parsley
1 tablespoon heavy cream
⅛ teaspoon rosemary
2 teaspoons seasoned bread
    crumbs, for topping

1. Preheat oven to 400°F and prepare 4 regular muffin cups by spraying with cooking spray.

2. Place 1 ham slice in each cup, pressing down to fill the cup. Allow any excess to fold into the cup.

3. Mix chicken, cheese, salt, pepper, mustard, parsley, cream, and rosemary.

4. Divide chicken mixture among cups, and sprinkle bread crumbs on top. Spray tops with cooking spray.

5. Bake for 12–15 minutes until chicken is cooked through. Refer to the "Meat Temperature Chart" in the Introduction for doneness.

Chicken cordon bleu is turned inside out when the ham acts as a cup for the dish. This is great with Savory Spinach Muffins (see Chapter 8).

CALORIES	132 calories
FAT	6.9 grams
PROTEIN	13.8 grams
SODIUM	498 mg
CARBOHYDRATES	2.3 grams
SUGARS	0.2 gram
FIBER	0.6 gram

peanut chicken with crunchy soba noodles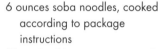

Makes 6

 Jumbo

6 ounces soba noodles, cooked according to package instructions

About 1 tablespoon sesame oil

1 small garlic clove, chopped

1 scallion, chopped

1 tablespoon olive oil

1 boneless, skinless chicken breast, cut into 1" pieces

½ teaspoon fresh grated gingerroot

½ cup broccoli florets

1 teaspoon chopped lemongrass (see sidebar)

2 tablespoons creamy peanut butter

1 teaspoon rice wine vinegar

1 tablespoon tamari sauce

½ cup chicken broth

1 tablespoon cornstarch

1. Preheat oven to 400°F and prepare 6 silicone jumbo muffin cup liners by spraying with cooking spray.

2. Divide soba noodles among cups and place 2–3 drops of sesame oil on each. Gently stir.

3. Bake for 20 minutes.

4. Cook garlic and scallion in olive oil for 1 minute, then add chicken breast, gingerroot, and broccoli and cook until the chicken is almost cooked through.

5. Add lemongrass and peanut butter. Continue cooking.

6. In a small bowl, whisk vinegar, tamari and chicken broth with cornstarch, then add to chicken mixture and cook until thickened.

7. Divide chicken mixture among muffin cups and bake for 7 minutes until heated through.

Soba noodles are made with buckwheat; you can find them in the Asian section of your supermarket. Lemongrass is the stalk of a plant, which, not surprisingly, has a lemony flavor. You can buy it fresh in the produce section, but I like to buy it minced in a squeeze tube. It lasts longer and is very easy to use. If you buy it fresh, peel off the hard outer part, and mince the soft inner part. You can substitute crunchy peanut butter for the creamy peanut butter if that's what you have on hand.

CALORIES	133 calories
FAT	7.3 grams
PROTEIN	7.7 grams
SODIUM	244 mg
CARBOHYDRATES	9.9 grams
SUGARS	0.8 gram
FIBER	0.9 gram

chicken and biscuits

Makes 10

1 boneless, skinless chicken breast
1 teaspoon olive oil
1 tablespoon butter
2 tablespoons plus ½ teaspoon flour
1¼ cups chicken broth
⅛ teaspoon onion powder
⅛ teaspoon dried rosemary
⅛ teaspoon poultry seasoning
1 tablespoon chopped fresh parsley
10 regular refrigerated canned biscuits

1. Preheat oven to 400°F and prepare 10 regular muffin cups.

2. Cook chicken breast in oil over medium heat until cooked through, then remove from pan. Once it is cool enough to handle, shred the chicken and set aside.

3. Using the same pan with the drippings, add butter and flour and cook until combined.

4. Whisk in chicken broth and stir in onion powder, rosemary, and poultry seasoning. Cook until thickened.

5. Stir in the shredded chicken.

6. Press one biscuit into each tin, pressing so it comes about ¾ up the sides.

7. Fill with chicken mixture.

8. Bake for 13 minutes until the biscuit is cooked through.

Chicken and biscuits is one of my favorite meals, and this version now makes it easier and more accessible than ever. Enjoy with Stewed Tomato Cups (see Chapter 7).

CALORIES	141 calories
FAT	5.6 grams
PROTEIN	4.9 grams
SODIUM	375 mg
CARBOHYDRATES	16.4 grams
SUGARS	3 grams
FIBER	0.7 gram

chicken fettuccine

Makes 8 or 9

 Regular

6 ounces fettuccine, cooked according to package instructions
¾ cup cream, divided
1 cup shredded Parmesan cheese, divided
Salt and pepper
½ a garlic clove
1 tablespoon unsalted butter
2 ounces light cream cheese
Pinch of nutmeg
1 tablespoon chopped fresh parsley
1 boneless, skinless chicken breast, cooked and cut into 1" pieces.

1. Preheat oven to 400°F, and prepare 8 or 9 regular muffin cups by spraying with cooking spray or lining with silicone liners (with liners you'll fill about 9; without, about 8).

2. Place fettuccine, ¼ cup cream, ¼ cup Parmesan, and salt and pepper to taste in a food processor and blend until it forms a sticky paste with small pieces of pasta visible.

3. Press pasta mix into muffin cups, pressing up the sides.

4. Bake for 7 minutes.

5. Rub a skillet with the cut side of the garlic, then melt butter in it over medium heat.

6. Add cream cheese, ½ cup Parmesan, ½ cup cream, ¼ teaspoon salt, ⅛ teaspoon pepper, nutmeg, and parsley. Stir until thickened and cheese is melted.

7. Add chicken and divide among cups.

8. Sprinkle remaining Parmesan on top and bake for about 7 minutes until bubbly and slightly brown on top and chicken is cooked through.

I love inside-out dishes like this, which combine all the flavors of the classic dish, but present them in a new and fun way. You could use shrimp in this dish instead of chicken, if you prefer.

CALORIES	202 calories (assuming recipe makes 8 servings)
FAT	13.8 grams
PROTEIN	10 grams
SODIUM	251 mg
CARBOHYDRATES	8.4 grams
SUGARS	0.7 gram
FIBER	0.4 gram

Chapter 5

Seafood

Seafood cooks beautifully in muffin tins, and makes it easy to create flavorful and exciting dishes that will entice you to enjoy the bounty of the sea in your diet more often. This chapter contains recipes for shrimp, crab, and different types of fish that you can enjoy cooked in individual muffin cups.

salmon noodle bake

Makes 10

 Regular

6 ounces salmon fillet, cooked
   and flaked
2 cups egg noodles, cooked
¼ cup heavy cream
Green part of a scallion,
   chopped
¼ cup soft light cream cheese
¼ cup green beans, cut into ½"
   pieces
¼ teaspoon dill weed
1 teaspoon lemon juice
1 egg
⅛ teaspoon onion powder

1. Preheat oven to 400°F and prepare 10 regular muffin cups by lining with foil or silicone liners.

2. Mix all ingredients together in a bowl completely.

3. Divide among muffin cups and bake for 12 minutes until cakes are set.

Similar to a tuna noodle casserole, this dish incorporates fresh cooked salmon, noodles, green beans, and cream cheese to create a tasty entrée.

CALORIES	115 calories
FAT	5.8 grams
PROTEIN	6.5 grams
SODIUM	59 mg
CARBOHYDRATES	9 grams
SUGARS	0.6 gram
FIBER	0.5 gram

tilapia with bok choy and loganberry

Makes 4

Jumbo

2 tilapia fillets
1 head baby bok choy (substitute spinach if preferred)
1 tablespoon olive oil
1 tablespoon loganberry syrup
1 teaspoon lemon juice
1 teaspoon tamari (or soy sauce)
½ teaspoon grated fresh gingerroot
Pepper to taste

1. Preheat oven to 400°F, and line 4 jumbo muffin cups with foil liners.

2. Cut each tilapia fillet in half the long way, then again the short way, for a total of 8 pieces.

3. Place 1 of the thinner pieces in each cup.

4. Divide the bok choy among the cups, breaking the leaves in half to fit if needed.

5. Top with remaining fish.

6. In a small bowl, mix oil, syrup, juice, tamari, gingerroot, and pepper.

7. Divide among the cups.

8. Bake for about 13 minutes, or until the fish is cooked through.

Loganberry syrup is a specialty in my hometown. Loganberry drinks were a staple at the now-defunct Crystal Beach amusement park, but you can still buy loganberry in a soda bottle or the syrup to make your own drink (Amazon.com sells PJ's Crystal Beach Loganberry Syrup). If you do pick up a bottle of syrup, follow the instructions to make your own beverages, or use it over shaved ice for a treat. You can substitute another fruit syrup if you prefer.

CALORIES	88 calories
FAT	1.2 grams
PROTEIN	15.4 grams
SODIUM	128 mg
CARBOHYDRATES	3.5 grams
SUGARS	2.6 grams
FIBER	0.4 gram

shrimp and pesto in phyllo

Makes 6

Regular

6 sheets of phyllo dough
½ pound raw shrimp, cleaned
and chopped
¼ cup pesto sauce

1. Preheat oven to 400°F and spray 6 regular muffin cups with cooking spray.

2. Cutting through all 6 sheets of phyllo, create 6 squares that are roughly 4½" or 5" on each side.

3. Place the stacks of phyllo squares in the cups, leaving the corners hanging over.

4. Spray the insides of the phyllo cups with cooking spray.

5. Mix shrimp and pesto and divide among cups.

6. Fold the corners of phyllo in over the shrimp, and spray the tops with cooking spray.

7. Bake for 10 minutes until shrimp is cooked through.

Phyllo dough creates a flaky and crisp cup for this dish. You can make your own pesto or buy it prepared in a jar.

CALORIES	93 calories
FAT	4.6 grams
PROTEIN	7.2 grams
SODIUM	440 mg
CARBOHYDRATES	13 grams
SUGARS	0.4 gram
FIBER	0.6 gram

very veggie tuna noodle casserole

Makes 18

 Regular

3 cups whole wheat egg noodles, cooked until al dente

1 6-ounce can of light tuna in water, drained

1 can condensed cream of mushroom soup

¼ cup frozen chopped spinach, drained

½ cup roughly chopped very tops of broccoli florets

½ cup shredded cheddar cheese

Salt and pepper to taste

1 teaspoon Italian herb mix

6 cherry tomatoes, roughly chopped

2 baby bella or button mushrooms, roughly chopped

2 green onions, roughly chopped

¼ cup skim milk

¼ cup heavy cream

¼ cup grated Parmesan cheese

8 saltines or other crackers

1. Preheat oven to 350°F. Prepare regular muffin tins by lining 18 cups with foil or silicone liners.

2. Mix all ingredients except crackers in a large bowl.

3. Using an ice cream scoop, fill the cups with the mixture.

4. Crush the crackers, and sprinkle on top, then spray with cooking spray.

5. Bake for 25 minutes until cooked through and golden on top.

This isn't your mom's tuna noodle casserole! The colorful and delicious vegetables make this delectable and appealing.

CALORIES	114 calories
FAT	4.1 grams
PROTEIN	7 grams
SODIUM	236 mg
CARBOHYDRATES	11.8 grams
SUGARS	0.8 gram
FIBER	1.4 grams

crab cakes with lemon mayo sauce

Makes 10

 Regular

5 tablespoons seasoned bread crumbs, plus additional for topping

1 pound jumbo lump crabmeat, picked over

2 eggs

Salt and pepper, to taste

¼ teaspoon Old Bay seasoning

½ teaspoon dried dill weed

4 teaspoons lemon juice

½ cup light mayonnaise

Lemon Mayo Sauce

½ cup light mayonnaise

2 tablespoons lemon juice

½ teaspoon dried dill

Ground pepper to taste

1. Preheat oven to 400°F, and prepare 10 regular muffin cups with foil or silicone liners.

2. Spray the liners with cooking spray, then sprinkle ½ tablespoon of bread crumbs in each and shake to coat bottom and sides.

3. Mix the rest of the ingredients in a bowl.

4. Divide among the muffin cups.

5. Sprinkle the tops with a pinch of bread crumbs on each, then spray with cooking spray.

6. Bake for 12–13 minutes until hot throughout and set and serve with Lemon Mayo Sauce.

Lemon Mayo Sauce

1. Mix and serve.

Enjoy these crab cakes as is, with the sauce on the side, or put them on a bun with the sauce slathered on and some lettuce and tomato as toppers. Either way, they are fresh and delicious tasting.

CALORIES	164 calories
FAT	8.9 grams
PROTEIN	10.9 grams
SODIUM	539 mg
CARBOHYDRATES	8.2 grams
SUGARS	1.7 grams
FIBER	0.5 gram

halibut and broccoli with brown butter

Makes 6

 Jumbo

2 cups cooked broccoli crowns
  (or frozen, thawed)
12 ounce halibut fillet, cut into
  6 pieces
6 tablespoons butter
2 teaspoons lemon juice
Salt and pepper

1. Preheat oven to 400°F and prepare 6 cups in a jumbo muffin tin with silicone or foil liners.

2. Divide the broccoli among the cups, and top with the fish.

3. Cook the butter in the microwave (covered, so it doesn't spatter) for 2–3 minutes until it becomes a nutty brown.

4. Carefully stir the lemon juice into butter (it will spit).

5. Divide butter among cups, then season fish with salt and pepper.

6. Bake for about 10 minutes (depending on thickness of fish) until fish is cooked through.

You can use any white firm fish in this recipe, such as cod or mahi-mahi. The brown butter gives the dish a complex taste, but it is very simple to make.

CALORIES	183 calories
FAT	11.6 grams
PROTEIN	14.1 grams
SODIUM	93 mg
CARBOHYDRATES	3.9 grams
SUGARS	0.8 gram
FIBER	1.7 grams

salmon in yogurt sauce over zucchini-rice cakes

Makes 4

Regular

⅓ cup shredded zucchini
⅓ cup cooked rice
1 tablespoon olive oil
Salt and pepper, to taste
1 6-ounce salmon fillet, cut into
    8 pieces
¼ cup plain Greek-style low-fat
    or fat-free yogurt
1 teaspoon lemon juice
½ teaspoon dried dill weed

1. Preheat oven to 400°F, and prepare 4 regular muffin cups by spraying with cooking spray.

2. Mix zucchini, rice, oil, salt, and pepper in a bowl, then divide among muffin cups, pressing into the bottoms.

3. Bake for 12 minutes.

4. Mix all other ingredients, with salt and pepper to taste in a bowl and divide among muffin cups, making sure there are 2 salmon pieces in each cup.

5. Bake for 10 minutes until salmon is cooked through.

I prefer to use only wild-caught salmon, as opposed to farmed salmon, because it contains less fat and fewer chemicals such as PCBs and mercury. Use brown rice for additional fiber.

CALORIES	145 calories
FAT	8.2 grams
PROTEIN	11.4 grams
SODIUM	68 mg
CARBOHYDRATES	4.8 grams
SUGARS	0.9 gram
FIBER	0.2 gram

greek shrimp cups

Makes 8

 Regular

8 sheets phyllo dough
½ pound shrimp, cleaned and chopped
8 frozen artichoke heart quarters, defrosted
½ 14.5-ounce can stewed tomatoes, juice and tomatoes separated
2 teaspoons cornstarch
1 tablespoon olive oil
1 tablespoon lemon juice
1 teaspoon Greek seasoning
1 small garlic clove, chopped
¼ teaspoon onion powder
¼ cup feta cheese

1. Preheat oven to 350°F, and prepare 8 regular muffin cups by spraying with cooking spray.

2. Stack the phyllo sheets, and cut them into 8 squares that are about 4" to 5" on each side. Place phyllo dough in the cups, corners hanging over.

3. Mix shrimp and artichoke hearts.

4. Chop tomatoes and add to shrimp-and-artichoke mixture.

5. Whisk tomato juice and cornstarch and add to shrimp-and-artichoke mixture.

6. Add all other ingredients and stir well.

7. Divide among cups and flip the corners of the phyllo dough in, then spray the tops of the phyllo with cooking spray.

8. Bake for 20 minutes until shrimp is cooked through.

You can use chunks of chicken breast instead of shrimp in this dish as well. Fat-free feta cheese is another great substitution.

CALORIES	180 calories
FAT	3.9 grams
PROTEIN	9.6 grams
SODIUM	398 mg
CARBOHYDRATES	26.3 grams
SUGARS	1.5 grams
FIBER	11.1 grams

salmon and rice cakes

Makes 7

 Regular

6 ounces salmon fillet, cooked
    and flaked
1 egg
1½ cups cooked brown rice
1 teaspoon grated fresh
    gingerroot
2 tablespoons tamari sauce
½ teaspoon rice vinegar
Green part of one scallion,
    chopped
1 teaspoon sesame oil

1. Preheat oven to 400°F and prepare 7 regular muffin cups by spraying with cooking spray.

2. Place all ingredients in a bowl and mix thoroughly.

3. Divide among muffin cups and bake for 9–10 minutes, until the cakes are set and slightly brown.

Tamari is like a thicker and richer soy sauce. It packs more flavor. You can substitute soy sauce for it, if you prefer. If you have leftover take-out fried rice, substitute it for the rice, for even more flavor.

CALORIES	115 calories
FAT	4.3 grams
PROTEIN	7.8 grams
SODIUM	312 mg
CARBOHYDRATES	10.5 grams
SUGARS	0.2 gram
FIBER	0.9 gram

creamy shrimp in puff pastry

Makes 9

 Regular

1 shallot, minced
1 celery stalk, minced
2 tablespoons unsalted butter
1 tablespoon Wondra flour
1 cup heavy cream
¼ teaspoon dried dill weed
Pinch of Old Bay seasoning
Pinch of nutmeg
1 tablespoon lemon juice
1 sheet frozen puff pastry,
    defrosted
12 shrimp, peeled, deveined

1. Preheat oven to 400°F, and prepare 9 cups in a regular muffin tin.

2. Cook shallots and celery in butter until softened.

3. Add flour and stir, cooking for about 1 minute.

4. Whisk in cream, dill weed, Old Bay, nutmeg, and lemon juice, stirring until sauce is thickened.

5. Allow sauce to cool.

6. Roll out the puff pastry until it forms a square big enough for you to cut out 9 circles of about 4½" in diameter. You should be able to fit 3 rows of 3 circles each.

7. Cut out the circles and place them in the muffin cups.

8. Cut the shrimp into thirds, then stir into sauce.

9. Divide among muffin cups.

10. Bake for 19 minutes until bubbling and until the puff pastry puffs and is golden brown.

Old Bay is a spice mix that is made especially to enhance seafood. You can find it in the spice aisle of your supermarket.

CALORIES	153 calories
FAT	13.6 grams
PROTEIN	2.2 grams
SODIUM	75 mg
CARBOHYDRATES	4.4 grams
SUGARS	0.2 gram
FIBER	0.2 gram

tuna burgers

Makes 6

2 6-ounce cans of chunk light tuna in water, drained

1 egg

1 tablespoon capers plus 1 tablespoon juice

1 tablespoon lemon juice

⅛ teaspoon pepper

1 small clove garlic

¼ cup light mayonnaise

3 tablespoons panko

1 tablespoon fresh chopped parsley

⅛ teaspoon salt

⅛ teaspoon dry mustard

1 tablespoon olive oil

¼ teaspoon sugar

1. Preheat oven to 400°F, and prepare 6 regular muffin cups by spraying with cooking spray.

2. Combine all ingredients in the food processor.

3. Divide among muffin cups, and bake for about 18 minutes, until cooked through and solid.

4. Serve on a bun with lettuce, tomato, and mayonnaise, or in a pita with a veggie salad.

If you've only had tuna as a cold sandwich spread or in a casserole, this is a new and fun way to do something with that can in your pantry! If you aren't worried about calories and fat, buy tuna packed in oil for a deeper flavor.

CALORIES	145 calories (burger only)
FAT	7.5 grams
PROTEIN	14.8 grams
SODIUM	392 mg
CARBOHYDRATES	1.8 grams
SUGARS	0.7 gram
FIBER	0.1 gram

cod and bok choy

Makes 6

Jumbo

2 heads baby bok choy, cleaned and roughly chopped
1 small garlic clove, minced
½ teaspoon sesame oil
¼ teaspoon fresh grated gingerroot
1 tablespoon olive oil
1 tablespoon lemon juice
1 tablespoon tamari sauce
12 ounces cod, cut into 6 pieces

1. Preheat the oven to 350°F and prepare 6 jumbo muffin cups with foil or silicone liners.

2. Place the bok choy in the bottoms of the cups.

3. Mix garlic, sesame oil, ginger, olive oil, lemon juice, and tamari in a small bowl. Sprinkle half of this over the bok choy.

4. Place cod on top of bok choy and sprinkle remaining sauce on top.

5. Bake for 8–10 minutes, depending on thickness of fish, until fish is completely cooked.

A friend who recently returned from Japan told me that this dish is one of the most commonly served in Japan. It's easy to prepare yet has lots of flavor. Serve this with some rice and Baked Veggie Stir-Fry (see Chapter 7).

CALORIES	70 calories
FAT	0.8 gram
PROTEIN	13.9 grams
SODIUM	227 mg
CARBOHYDRATES	1.3 grams
SUGARS	0.2 gram
FIBER	0.5 gram

salmon cakes

Makes 10

 Regular

12 ounces salmon fillet
½ teaspoon dried dill weed
½ cup panko
½ cup crème fraiche, plus additional for serving
1 egg
⅛ teaspoon dry mustard
Green part of a scallion, chopped
¼ cup seasoned bread crumbs, plus 1 teaspoon for topping
Salt and pepper, to taste
1 tablespoon chopped fresh parsley

1. Preheat oven to 400°F and prepare 10 regular muffin cups with cooking spray.

2. Place salmon on a baking sheet and bake for 8–12 minutes, depending on thickness, until cooked.

3. Place salmon in a bowl and flake with a fork.

4. Add all other ingredients.

5. Mix with a fork to combine.

6. Divide among muffin cups, filling about ¾ full.

7. Divide additional 1 teaspoon bread crumbs by sprinkling on tops of salmon cakes, then spray the tops with cooking spray.

8. Bake for 10 minutes until the cakes are set and slightly golden.

Serve with extra crème fraiche and some rice. You can also serve these on buns as sandwiches.

CALORIES	100 calories
FAT	8.9 grams
PROTEIN	9.3 grams
SODIUM	111 mg
CARBOHYDRATES	3.5 grams
SUGARS	0.2 gram
FIBER	0.2 gram

scallop gratin

Makes 6

 Regular

1 pound bay scallops (see sidebar)
¼ cup seasoned bread crumbs, plus additional reserved for topping
Salt and pepper, to taste
1 tablespoon lemon juice
¼ teaspoon dried dill weed
¼ cup heavy cream
1 teaspoon cornstarch

1. Preheat oven to 400°F and prepare 6 regular muffin cups with silicone or foil liners.

2. Mix all ingredients together in a bowl, combining completely.

3. Divide among muffin cups, and place a pinch of bread crumbs on top of each, then spray with cooking spray.

4. Bake for 8 minutes, then broil for 4 minutes until brown and bubbly.

Tiny bay scallops are the perfect size for these personal-size gratins. Be sure to rinse the scallops first to remove any grit or sand. Be careful not to overcook these.

CALORIES	139 calories
FAT	4.1 grams
PROTEIN	16.5 grams
SODIUM	619 mg
CARBOHYDRATES	8.4 grams
SUGARS	0.4 gram
FIBER	0.3 gram

fish tacos

Makes 6

Jumbo

3 pieces tilapia, about 3–4 ounces each, cut in half
¼ teaspoon chili powder
¼ cup fresh chopped cilantro
1 tablespoon olive oil
2 tablespoons lime juice
Salt and pepper
6 taco-size flour tortillas
Light sour cream, chopped green onion, chopped tomato, lettuce, and salsa for serving

1. Place the tilapia, chili powder, cilantro, oil, lime juice, and salt and pepper in a bowl and allow to marinate ½ an hour, in the refrigerator.

2. Preheat oven to 400°F and prepare 6 jumbo muffin cups by spraying with cooking spray.

3. Push one taco tortilla down into each cup and press any sections that bubble out against the sides.

4. Place 1 piece of marinated tilapia in each cup and bake for 10 to 12 minutes, depending on thickness of fish, until cooked through.

5. Serve with toppings.

Taco tortillas are smaller tortillas and are just the right size to line jumbo muffin cups. Lemon juice can be substituted for lime juice.

CALORIES	178 calories (without toppings)
FAT	6.1 grams
PROTEIN	16.2 grams
SODIUM	66 mg
CARBOHYDRATES	11.1 grams
SUGARS	0.3 gram
FIBER	1.6 grams

deviled crab tarts

Makes 12

 Regular

12 slices sandwich bread
½ medium onion, chopped
½ celery rib, chopped
¼ red bell pepper, chopped
2 tablespoons unsalted butter
¾ cup lump crabmeat, picked
   over
1 tablespoon chopped fresh
   parsley
2 teaspoons lemon juice
½ cup light mayonnaise
¼ cup seasoned bread crumbs
1 tablespoon Worcestershire
   sauce
Pinch cayenne pepper
¼ teaspoon salt
⅛ teaspoon ground black
   pepper
½ green part of a scallion,
   chopped

1. Preheat oven to 400°F and prepare 12 regular muffin cups by spraying with cooking spray.

2. Remove crust from bread, and press 1 piece into each muffin cup, pressing to fit and pressing tight into the sides and bottom.

3. Spray bread with cooking spray.

4. Bake for 10 minutes until bread is golden and crisp.

5. Mix all other ingredients together and divide among muffin cups.

6. Bake 8 minutes until tarts are completely hot.

Baking the bread creates a crunchy crust for this crab tart and makes a nice change from pastry crust. These work as entrées or appetizers.

CALORIES	150 calories
FAT	5.7 grams
PROTEIN	4 grams
SODIUM	342 mg
CARBOHYDRATES	16 grams
SUGARS	2.1 grams
FIBER	1 gram

salmon pie

Makes 4

 Jumbo

1 can crescent roll dough (8 pieces)
½ small onion, chopped
1 tablespoon butter
2 tablespoons Wondra flour
1 14.5-ounce can stewed tomatoes
¼ cup white wine
1 tablespoon chopped fresh parsley
6 ounces salmon fillet, cooked and then broken or flaked into small pieces
½ cup green beans, cut into 1" pieces and blanched (or use frozen beans that have been thawed)
¼ cup frozen peas, thawed
¼ teaspoon salt
¼ teaspoon pepper
⅛ teaspoon paprika
¼ cup shredded good quality sharp white cheddar cheese
¼ teaspoon celery salt

1. Preheat oven to 400°F and prepare 4 jumbo muffin cups.

2. Open the tube of crescent rolls. Press 2 triangles together to form a solid rectangle. Continue until you have 4 rectangles.

3. Place each rectangle in a muffin cup, and press it down to the bottom and press the sides around so they cover the inside of the cup.

4. Cook onion and butter in a large skillet over medium high heat until onion is translucent.

5. Stir in flour and cook for 30 seconds.

6. Add tomatoes and cook, stirring, breaking them up into small pieces.

7. Add wine and cook until thickened and tomatoes are softened and broken up.

8. Add remaining ingredients, stirring until combined.

9. Divide among muffin cups and bake for about 20 minutes until crescent dough is golden.

This dish is based on a recipe the Asa Ransom House in Clarence, New York, used to serve, called Salmon Pond Pie. It's like a salmon potpie.

CALORIES	412 calories
FAT	22 grams
PROTEIN	18 grams
SODIUM	860 mg
CARBOHYDRATES	35.7 grams
SUGARS	7.1 grams
FIBER	3.1 grams

tilapia florentine

Makes 8

 Regular

1 tube refrigerated crescent roll
   dough (8 pieces)
2 tilapia fillets, 4–6 ounces each
½ cup canned diced tomatoes,
   with juice
½ cup packed chopped fresh
   escarole
Salt and pepper to taste
½ teaspoon Italian seasoning
4 teaspoons lemon juice
¼ cup capers

1. Preheat oven to 400°F and prepare 8 regular muffin cups.

2. Follow the instructions for crescent rolls in "Crescent Roll Crusts" in the Introduction to prepare crescent roll dough. Place in muffin cups.

3. Cut fish into 16 equal pieces.

4. Mix fish and remaining ingredients in a bowl.

5. Divide among muffin cups, being sure to place 2 pieces of fish in each cup.

6. Bake for 12–15 minutes until bubbly and crescent roll is golden.

Tilapia is a very versatile fish that takes on the flavor of the ingredients it is cooked with. And it is considered sustainable when it is farmed in the United States.

CALORIES	156 calories
FAT	6.9 grams
PROTEIN	11.5 grams
SODIUM	407 mg
CARBOHYDRATES	12.1 grams
SUGARS	3.5 grams
FIBER	0.4 gram

shrimp with polenta

Makes 6

 Jumbo

2¾ cups water
1 cup cornmeal
Salt and pepper
4 tablespoons unsalted butter, divided
1 small clove garlic, chopped
¾ pound shrimp, peeled
1 teaspoon fresh rosemary
2 teaspoons Worcestershire sauce
1 teaspoon lemon juice
1 teaspoon cornstarch
1 tablespoon chopped fresh parsley

1. Bring water to a boil then add cornmeal and dash of salt. Reduce heat to low and simmer for about 15 minutes, until thick.

2. Stir in 1 tablespoon butter. Take off heat and set polenta aside.

3. Preheat oven to 400°F and prepare 6 jumbo muffin cups with silicone or foil liners.

4. Divide polenta among cups, filling about halfway.

5. Brown 3 tablespoons of butter in the microwave, then stir in garlic and allow to cool a few minutes.

6. Place shrimp in a bowl and add butter-garlic mixture, rosemary, Worcestershire, lemon juice, cornstarch, parsley, and salt and pepper to taste.

7. Divide among cups, using all the sauce.

8. Bake for 10–12 minutes, until the shrimp is cooked through.

This taste of the South will hit the spot. Serve with Minestrone Pie (see Chapter 7).

CALORIES	180 calories
FAT	8 grams
PROTEIN	9.5 grams
SODIUM	376 mg
CARBOHYDRATES	17.2 grams
SUGARS	0.4 gram
FIBER	1.5 grams

Chapter 6

Potatoes, Rice, Pizza, and Pasta

No more pans to scrub! Make your potato, rice, and pasta dishes in muffin cups with liners, and your cleanup becomes simpler. Muffin cups also work well for mini pizzas and nicely portioned individual servings of rice sides.

duchess potatoes

Makes 6

 Regular

5 medium Yukon Gold potatoes
1 tablespoon unsalted butter
1 tablespoon olive oil
1 egg white
Salt and pepper, to taste
2 tablespoons Parmesan cheese, plus 1 tablespoon reserved
¼ tablespoon onion powder
1½ tablespoons chopped parsley
1 tablespoon skim milk
Pinch of paprika

1. Preheat oven to 350°F.

2. Place 6 foil or silicone muffin tin liners in a regular muffin tin.

3. Spray the insides with cooking spray.

4. Prick the potatoes and cook them in the microwave until tender, about 3 minutes.

5. Allow to cool for a few minutes, then pull the skin off them.

6. Place potatoes in a food processor and add all ingredients except reserved cheese and paprika. Pulse until smooth. If you do not have a food processor, mash the potatoes with a masher until fairly smooth, then mash in other ingredients, other than reserved cheese and paprika.

7. Fill the cups to the top.

8. Top with reserved cheese and a tiny pinch of paprika on each one.

9. Bake for 15 minutes until golden.

These creamy potatoes puff up when cooked to be lighter than mashed potatoes. They go well with beef dishes.

CALORIES	143 calories
FAT	4.8 grams
PROTEIN	4.6 grams
SODIUM	80 mg
CARBOHYDRATES	21.1 grams
SUGARS	2.7 grams
FIBER	2.5 grams

skinny pizza cups

Maker 12

 Regular

4 whole wheat tortillas

½ cup shredded part-skim mozzarella cheese

6 ounces chopped frozen spinach, thawed and squeezed dry

12 pieces turkey pepperoni

4 white or baby bella mushrooms, sliced

1 cup spaghetti sauce

¼ cup grated cheddar cheese (such as San Joaquin Gold)

1. Preheat oven to 350°F.

2. Line a regular muffin tin with 12 liners.

3. Lay the tortillas on a cutting board, on top of each other.

4. Cut 4½" circles from the tortillas, making 3 circles from each tortilla or 12 in total.

5. Place 1 circle of tortilla in each muffin cup liner, pressing down so it fits inside.

6. Place the mozzarella cheese in the tortilla.

7. Top with spinach, pepperoni, and mushrooms.

8. Then pour sauce on top, and sprinkle the top with the grated cheddar cheese.

9. Bake for 15 minutes, until cheese has melted and cups are slightly bubbly.

Make this dish vegetarian by leaving out the pepperoni. Use up the unused pieces of tortilla by baking with a little unsalted butter and cinnamon sugar, for a crispy treat.

CALORIES	52 calories
FAT	2.75 grams
PROTEIN	5.3 grams
SODIUM	326.5 mg
CARBOHYDRATES	12.7 grams
SUGARS	2.8 grams
FIBER	42.1 grams

candied yams

Makes 8

 Regular

2 large yams
3 tablespoons melted unsalted butter
½ teaspoon vanilla
½ teaspoon salt
¼ cup brown sugar
1 egg
½ teaspoon cinnamon
1 tablespoon heavy cream
50–60 mini marshmallows

1. Preheat oven to 400°F and prepare 8 regular muffin cups with silicone or foil liners.

2. Cook yams in microwave (prick with a fork first), until soft, about 4–6 minutes.

3. Remove skins and mash the yams.

4. Add all other ingredients except marshmallows and mix completely.

5. Divide among muffin cups and top each with 6–8 marshmallows.

6. Bake for 25 minutes until browned.

Enjoy your candied yams with the portion size predetermined. These bake up smooth and sweet.

CALORIES	119 calories
FAT	5.3 grams
PROTEIN	1.4 grams
SODIUM	159 mg
CARBOHYDRATES	16.3 grams
SUGARS	6.9 grams
FIBER	1.3 grams

Smoky Popcorn Cheese Snacks • Chapter 1

Corned Beef Hash Cups • Chapter 2

Taco Mini Pies • Chapter 3

Chicken Florentine Meatloaf • Chapter 4

Mango Tandoori Chicken • Chapter 4

Skinny Pizza Cups • Chapter 6

Blueberry Mini Pies • Chapter 8

Spice-Rubbed Pork Tenderloin • Chapter 3

Tortellini in Ham Cups • Chapter 6

French Onion Pie • Chapter 7

Tomato Pie • Chapter 7

Strawberry Trifle • Chapter 8

Reuben Pies • Chapter 3

Egg Crescent Pockets • Chapter 2

Left to Right: Spice-Rubbed Pork Tenderloin, Blueberry Mini Pie, and Black-Bottom Strawberry Cheesecake

Halibut and Broccoli with Brown Butter • Chapter 5

Salmon Pie • Chapter 5

linguine nests

Makes 6

 Jumbo

¼ cup plus 2 tablespoons pesto
¼ cup plus 2 tablespoons light cream cheese
¾ cup tomato sauce
Salt and pepper to taste
3 tablespoons olive oil
¾ cup grated Parmesan cheese, plus more for serving
¼ cup plus 2 tablespoons chopped mushrooms
¾ cup chopped broccoli
6 refrigerated fresh linguine nests
¼ cup plus 2 tablespoons water

1. Preheat oven to 350°F.

2. Prepare 6 jumbo muffin cups by spraying with cooking spray.

3. Mix all ingredients except pasta and water in a bowl.

4. Place 1 tablespoon of pesto mixture in the bottom of each cup.

5. Plunge linguini nests in boiling water for 2 minutes. Place a nest in each cup.

6. Place 2 tablespoons water in each cup.

7. Divide pesto mixture among cups, moving the pasta around to mix pesto into the nest.

8. Cover the muffin tin with foil and bake for 15 minutes.

9. Remove from oven, remove foil, and stir each nest so the sauce gets distributed evenly.

10. Recover with foil and return to oven for 10 more minutes until pasta is tender.

11. Serve with additional grated Parmesan cheese.

Fresh, refrigerated pasta is already soft, so it cooks very quickly. You could add meatballs to these to make a meat entrée.

CALORIES	193 calories
FAT	11.9 grams
PROTEIN	10.8 grams
SODIUM	608 mg
CARBOHYDRATES	23.3 grams
SUGARS	4.7 grams
FIBER	1.8 grams

twice-baked stuffed potatoes

Maker 4

 Jumbo

2 large baking potatoes, cooked
    and cooled enough to handle
1 tablespoon melted unsalted
    butter
Salt and pepper
⅓ cup grated Gruyère cheese
⅓ cup light sour cream
⅓ cup cooked chopped broccoli
½ green part of a scallion,
    chopped
1 slice deli ham, chopped
Paprika

1. Preheat oven to 400°F and prepare 4 jumbo muffin cups by spraying with cooking spray.

2. Cut each potato in half the short way and then cut enough off the pointy end so that the potato can stand up.

3. Scoop out the insides of the potatoes, leaving enough intact so the potato holds its shape. Reserve potato flesh. Place potato shells in muffin cups.

4. In a bowl, place reserved potato flesh. Add in butter, salt and pepper, Gruyère cheese, sour cream, broccoli, scallion, and ham. Mix until combined.

5. Stuff mixture into potato shells, mounding on top.

6. Sprinkle tops lightly with paprika.

7. Bake for 25 minutes until heated through and golden on top.

Standing the potatoes on their ends makes them fit perfectly in muffin cups. Play with the stuffing a bit for different flavors. You could use spinach or asparagus instead of broccoli, try different cheeses, or remove the ham.

CALORIES	188 calories
FAT	8.1 grams
PROTEIN	7.2 grams
SODIUM	188 mg
CARBOHYDRATES	21.3 grams
SUGARS	1.2 grams
FIBER	2.6 grams

hearty deep-dish pizzas

Makes 12

 Jumbo

28 ounces fresh refrigerated pizza dough

1½ cups pizza or spaghetti sauce

12 pieces of pepperoni or topping of your choice

1½ cups shredded part-skim mozzarella cheese

¼ cup shredded Parmesan cheese

1. Preheat oven to 400°F and prepare 12 jumbo muffin cups.

2. Cut the pizza dough into 12 equal pieces.

3. Shape each piece into a 6" circle and place each in a muffin cup, pressing to fit.

4. Place 2 tablespoons of sauce in each cup.

5. Add the pepperoni (or any other topping you are using).

6. Sprinkle 2 tablespoons mozzarella and 1 teaspoon Parmesan on top of each cup.

7. Bake for 17 minutes until dough is cooked and cheese is melted.

You can buy prepared pizza dough in the refrigerated deli case at your supermarket. Substitute anchovies for pepperoni, if you like, or substitute some different cheeses for the mozzarella.

CALORIES	252 calories
FAT	6.8 grams
PROTEIN	13.3 grams
SODIUM	807 mg
CARBOHYDRATES	31.1 grams
SUGARS	0.8 gram
FIBER	1.8 grams

maple sweet potato and kale

Makes 6

 Jumbo

2 cups tightly packed chopped kale
1 sweet potato or yam, peeled and cut into 6 rounds
2 tablespoons olive oil
2 tablespoons maple syrup
Salt and pepper

1. Preheat oven to 350°F and prepare 6 jumbo muffin tin cups with silicone liners.

2. Divide kale among muffin cups.

3. Place 1 round sweet potato slice on top of kale in each cup.

4. Drizzle olive oil and maple syrup on top, then season with salt and pepper.

5. Bake for 50 minutes, or until potatoes are cooked through.

Wondering what to do with kale? You know it's a healthy food but it can be a little tricky to cook with. This dish combines it with sweet potatoes for a lovely wintery dish.

CALORIES	89 calories
FAT	4.5 grams
PROTEIN	1.1 grams
SODIUM	46 mg
CARBOHYDRATES	11 grams
SUGARS	4.9 grams
FIBER	1.1 grams

savory noodle kugel

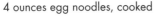

Makes 4

 Jumbo

4 ounces egg noodles, cooked
3 eggs
⅓ cup light sour cream
2 tablespoons melted unsalted
    butter
⅛ teaspoon pepper
¼ teaspoon salt
⅓ cup Boursin light garlic and
    herb cheese spread
¼ cup heavy cream
Pinch of sugar
1 tablespoon flour
⅛ teaspoon dry mustard
¼ cup shredded Asiago cheese
¼ cup crushed crackers

1. Preheat oven to 350°F and prepare 4 jumbo muffin cups with silicone or foil liners.

2. Combine all ingredients except crackers.

3. Divide among muffin tins.

4. Top with cracker crumbs and spray tops with cooking spray.

5. Bake for about 25 minutes until custard is set in the center.

Noodle kugel is usually a dessert, but I've changed things up and made this as a savory dish. This goes well with Stuffed Cube Steak (see Chapter 3).

CALORIES	306 calories
FAT	20.1 grams
PROTEIN	9.5 grams
SODIUM	458 mg
CARBOHYDRATES	14.7 grams
SUGARS	0.5 gram
FIBER	0.5 gram

butternut squash rice cups

Makes 12

 Regular

2 ounces chopped pancetta

2½ cups cooked brown rice

1 12-ounce package frozen butternut squash, thawed

½ teaspoon salt

¼ teaspoon pepper

1 tablespoon chopped fresh sage

2 teaspoons heavy cream

3½ ounces Monterey Jack cheese, cut into small cubes

½ cup shredded Parmesan cheese

1. Preheat oven to 400°F and prepare 12 regular muffin cups with silicone or foil liners.

2. Cook the pancetta in a skillet, until crisp. Remove the skillet from the heat, and drain off the fat.

3. Stir in rice and squash.

4. Add salt, pepper, sage, and cream and stir until combined.

5. Stir in Monterey Jack cheese and divide among muffin cups.

6. Sprinkle Parmesan cheese on the tops and bake for 15 minutes until lightly browned on top.

Pancetta is a smoky Italian bacon that adds lots of flavor to this dish. Using frozen butternut squash makes this dish a snap.

CALORIES	130 calories
FAT	5.7 grams
PROTEIN	5.8 grams
SODIUM	257 mg
CARBOHYDRATES	14.1 grams
SUGARS	0.9 gram
FIBER	1.1 grams

smashed red potato cakes

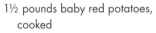

Makes 12

 Regular

1½ pounds baby red potatoes, cooked
⅔ cup light sour cream
4 tablespoons melted unsalted butter
Salt and pepper to taste
2 tablespoons chives, chopped
¼ cup shredded cheddar cheese
⅛ teaspoon onion powder
⅛ teaspoon smoked paprika
2 tablespoons grated Parmesan cheese
¼ cup plain low-fat or fat-free yogurt

1. Preheat oven to 400°F and prepare 12 regular muffin cups by spraying with cooking spray or lining with foil or silicone liners.

2. Peel the skins off half of the potatoes and discard; place potatoes in a bowl.

3. Add the rest of the potatoes. Smash with a fork.

4. Stir in all other ingredients.

5. Divide among muffin tins and bake for 17 minutes, until golden on top.

Faster and easier than mashed potatoes, this dish is made very colorful by the inclusion of some of the red skins.

CALORIES	107 calories
FAT	6 grams
PROTEIN	2.8 grams
SODIUM	62 mg
CARBOHYDRATES	10.4 grams
SUGARS	1.2 grams
FIBER	1 gram

mac and cheese cups

Makes 10

 Jumbo

1 box (14.5 ounces) whole
    wheat elbow macaroni
3 tablespoons unsalted butter
⅓ cup chopped onion
¼ cup flour
2 cups skim milk
⅛ teaspoon dry mustard
⅛ teaspoon ground pepper
⅛ teaspoon salt
Pinch cayenne pepper
Pinch nutmeg
2 slices prepackaged Velveeta
    cheese
1⅓ cups grated good quality
    sharp cheddar cheese
¾ cup grated fontina cheese
1 cup grated Swiss cheese
    (Emmentaler or another good
    quality)
¼ cup blue cheese
⅓ cup grated caraway Havarti
    cheese
⅓ cup grated Parmesan cheese,
    plus 3 tablespoons reserved
    for topping
2 tablespoons light sour cream
2 tablespoons seasoned bread
    crumbs

1. Cook macaroni according to package instructions, until al dente. Set aside.

2. Preheat oven to 400°F and prepare 10 jumbo muffin cups with foil or silicone liners (sprayed with cooking spray).

3. Melt butter in saucepan over medium heat. Add onion, cooking and stirring until onion is cooked through and just beginning to brown.

4. Stir in flour and cook about 1 minute.

5. Whisk in milk and cook until thickened.

6. Add seasonings, cheeses, and sour cream and stir until all cheese is melted and combined.

7. Stir in macaroni, and divide among muffin cups.

8. Divide bread crumbs among the cups, and spray with cooking spray.

9. Sprinkle reserved Parmesan cheese on top.

10. Bake 10 minutes until bubbling, then broil about 2 minutes until top is browned.

Although this looks like regular mac and cheese, the sophisticated mix of cheeses takes it to a new level. You can substitute any cheeses you would like in this recipe. For example, try using some smoked Gouda instead of the blue cheese, or Monterey Jack in place of the fontina.

CALORIES	390 calories
FAT	17.2 grams
PROTEIN	20.2 grams
SODIUM	440 mg
CARBOHYDRATES	38.8 grams
SUGARS	3.5 grams
FIBER	3.7 grams

potato parsnip cups

Makes 8

 Regular

1 baking potato (about 8
  ounces)
1 parsnip (about 6 ounces)
3 tablespoons melted unsalted
  butter
Salt and pepper to taste
2 tablespoons plain Greek low-
  fat or fat-free yogurt
2 tablespoons light sour cream
1 tablespoon heavy cream
1 tablespoon fresh chopped
  chives
2 tablespoons grated Gruyère
  cheese
2 tablespoons part-skim ricotta
  cheese

1. Preheat oven to 400°F and prepare 8 regular muffin cups
with silicone or foil liners.

2. Peel and thinly slice potato and parsnip and cook in pot
of boiling water until fork tender, 3–4 minutes, or longer if
your slices are not extremely thin. Drain off the water.

3. Mash the potato and parsnip and mix in all other
ingredients.

4. Divide among muffin cups and bake 15 minutes until
golden on top.

The parsnips give the potatoes a slightly sweet taste and serve to lighten
up the dish.

CALORIES	95 calories
FAT	5.5 grams
PROTEIN	2.3 grams
SODIUM	34 mg
CARBOHYDRATES	8.9 grams
SUGARS	1.3 grams
FIBER	1.1 grams

white pizzas

Makes 24

28 ounces fresh pizza dough
Cooking spray
½ cup pesto sauce
¾ cup chopped cooked chicken
12 frozen artichoke heart quarters, defrosted
½ cup shredded smoked mozzarella cheese
½ cup shredded fontinella cheese

1. Preheat oven to 400°F, and prepare 24 regular muffin cups.

2. Cut the pizza dough into 24 equal pieces.

3. Place each piece of dough in a cup and press it to get it to cover the inside of the cup.

4. Lightly spray the inside of each piece of dough with cooking spray.

5. Spread 1 teaspoon of pesto in each cup and top with ½ tablespoon chicken.

6. Cut the artichoke quarters in half, so you have 24 pieces. Add 1 piece to each cup.

7. Sprinkle 1 teaspoon smoked mozzarella and 1 teaspoon fontinella on each cup.

8. Bake for 12 minutes until dough is cooked and cheese has melted.

I love white pizzas because they are so versatile. You could use garlic and oil instead of pesto for sauce in this dish if you wish. Use broccoli or spinach instead of artichoke, or shrimp instead of chicken.

CALORIES	109 calories
FAT	3.2 grams
PROTEIN	4.8 grams
SODIUM	322 mg
CARBOHYDRATES	15.3 grams
SUGARS	0.3 gram
FIBER	1.3 grams

stuffed potato cups

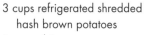

Makes 6

 Regular

3 cups refrigerated shredded
  hash brown potatoes
1 egg white
Salt and pepper, to taste
1 tablespoon olive oil
¼ cup finely chopped raw broccoli florets
¼ cup chopped ham
¼ cup light sour cream
¼ cup shredded sharp cheddar
  cheese
1 tablespoon chopped chives
1 tablespoon chopped green
  onion
Pinch of paprika

1. Preheat oven to 400°F. Use 6 cups in a regular nonstick muffin tin, unsprayed.

2. Mix potatoes, egg white, salt and pepper, and olive oil in a bowl.

3. Divide potatoes among muffin cups and press to form the shape of the cup, all the way to the top.

4. Bake for 25 minutes.

5. Mix remaining ingredients in a bowl, adding additional salt and pepper to taste.

6. Fill the cups with the mixture and return to the oven for about 15 minutes, until the cheese melts.

Use cooked crumbled bacon instead of ham, if you like. Try using plain low-fat or fat-free yogurt instead of light sour cream. You can make the potato cups and use them to hold other ingredients, like chicken in cream sauce or chipped beef.

CALORIES	151 calories
FAT	5.6 grams
PROTEIN	5.2 grams
SODIUM	156 mg
CARBOHYDRATES	20.1 grams
SUGARS	0.2 gram
FIBER	1.7 grams

wild rice frittatas

Makes 12

 Regular

⅓ cup cooked wild rice, still hot (or reheated)
⅔ cup cooked brown rice, still hot (or reheated)
2 tablespoons butter
2 eggs, divided
Green part of scallion, chopped
Salt and pepper, to taste
½ cup skim milk
¼ cup grated fontina cheese
1 tablespoon Parmesan cheese

1. Preheat oven to 400°F and prepare 12 regular muffin cups.

2. Mix hot rice with butter and allow to cool.

3. Mix in egg yolks, scallion, salt, pepper, milk, and fontina cheese.

4. Beat egg whites until they form stiff peaks, then fold into mixture.

5. Divide among muffin cups and top with Parmesan cheese.

6. Bake 15–18 minutes until set and golden on top.

Wild rice gives this dish a great crunch. You could stir in some broccoli or spinach, if you like.

CALORIES	60 calories
FAT	3.4 grams
PROTEIN	2.6 grams
SODIUM	54 mg
CARBOHYDRATES	4.2 grams
SUGARS	0.7 gram
FIBER	0.3 gram

yorkshire pudding

Makes 10

 Regular

5 teaspoons vegetable oil
1 cup flour
½ teaspoon salt
1 cup skim milk
2 eggs

1. Preheat oven to 425°F.

2. Using a regular muffin tin, place ½ teaspoon vegetable oil in each of 10 cups. Place in preheating oven.

3. In a bowl, mix the rest of the ingredients. The batter will be lumpy.

4. Divide among the 10 cups.

5. Bake for 10–12 minutes until golden and puffed.

Yorkshire pudding (which isn't a pudding in the American sense at all and is instead a baked batter) is a special treat at my house and I often have to double or triple the batch. In this recipe, the puddings are made in individual sizes and are similar to popovers, but with a crunchier bottom.

CALORIES	89 calories
FAT	3.3 grams
PROTEIN	3.3 grams
SODIUM	143 mg
CARBOHYDRATES	10.8 grams
SUGARS	1.3 grams
FIBER	0.3 gram

ravioli lasagna

Makes 6

 Jumbo

12 round ravioli, any kind
½ cup part-skim ricotta cheese
¼ teaspoon Italian seasoning
⅛ teaspoon garlic powder
Salt and pepper to taste
1 tablespoon skim milk
1 24-ounce jar spaghetti sauce
¾ cup shredded part-skim moz-
    zarella cheese
3 teaspoons grated Parmesan
    cheese

1. Preheat oven to 400°F and prepare 6 jumbo muffin cups with foil or silicone liners. Spray the liners with cooking spray.

2. Cook the ravioli according to package instructions until al dente.

3. In a small bowl, mix ricotta, Italian seasoning, garlic powder, salt, pepper, and milk.

4. Cut each ravioli in half, so you have two circles (it's okay if the filling ends up mostly on one side). (This step allows all the flavors to combine like a real lasagna.)

5. Place 2 teaspoons of spaghetti sauce in the bottom of each cup.

6. In each cup, layer ½ of a ravioli (skin side down), 1 teaspoon ricotta mix, 1 teaspoon mozzarella, and 2 teaspoons spaghetti sauce on top. Repeat this two more times in each cup.

7. Top each cup with ½ of a ravioli (skin side up).

8. Top with 2 teaspoons spaghetti sauce and ½ teaspoon Parmesan.

9. Bake for 15 minutes until bubbly. Allow to cool and set for a few minutes before you remove the cups from the muffin pan.

At last, lasagna made easy! Ravioli are the perfect base for lasagna made in muffin cups, providing not only the pasta, but the cheesy sauce.

CALORIES	233 calories
FAT	9.1 grams
PROTEIN	11.2 grams
SODIUM	688 mg
CARBOHYDRATES	26.5 grams
SUGARS	11 grams
FIBER	3.6 grams

tortellini in ham cups

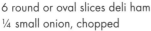

 Regular

6 round or oval slices deli ham
¼ small onion, chopped
1 tablespoon unsalted butter
½ teaspoon Italian seasoning
Salt and pepper
2 tablespoons Wondra flour
¼ cup chicken broth
¾ cup skim milk
¼ cup shredded fontina cheese
¼ cup shredded Parmesan cheese, plus ¼ cup for topping
9 ounces refrigerated tortellini, cooked according to package instructions

1. Preheat oven to 400°F and prepare 6 regular muffin cups by spraying with cooking spray or inserting silicone liners.

2. Place 1 slice of ham in each cup. Let the edges hang over.

3. Cook onion in butter over medium high heat until translucent, then stir in seasoning, salt, pepper, and Wondra and cook for 1 minute.

4. Stir in broth and milk and cook until thickened, about 2 minutes.

5. Stir in cheeses until melted.

6. Turn off heat and stir in tortellini.

7. Divide among cups and sprinkle tops with ¼ cup Parmesan cheese.

8. Bake for 12 minutes until heated through and slightly golden on top.

Make this dish different each time you make it by choosing tortellini with different fillings. Another variation is to use salami instead of ham to make the cups.

CALORIES	250 calories
FAT	9.2 grams
PROTEIN	14.7 grams
SODIUM	782 mg
CARBOHYDRATES	25.2 grams
SUGARS	2.2 grams
FIBER	1.4 grams

inside out samosas

Makes 12

Regular

4 cups refrigerated hash brown potato chunks
2 eggs
2 tablespoons cream
2 tablespoons seasoned bread crumbs
¼ teaspoon curry powder, plus ½ teaspoon for filling
1 cup frozen peas, thawed
½ teaspoon fresh grated gingerroot
1 large clove garlic, minced
½ cup plain low-fat or fat-free yogurt
2 tablespoons chopped green chiles (from a can)
1 teaspoon cornstarch

1. Preheat oven to 400°F and prepare 12 regular muffin cups by spraying with cooking spray.

2. Place potatoes, eggs, cream, bread crumbs, and curry powder in a food processor, and process until completely pulverized.

3. Divide the mixture among the cups, and press into the sides and bottoms of the cups. Spray with cooking spray.

4. Bake for 13 minutes.

5. Mix peas, gingerroot, garlic, additional curry powder, yogurt, chiles, and cornstarch in a bowl, and combine.

6. Divide among potato cups, and bake for 12 minutes until heated through and slightly golden on top.

Samosas are an Indian delight enjoyed throughout Asia, Africa, and the Middle East. They are usually a stuffed pastry filled with potatoes, peas, and spices. In this recipe, I've turned the samosa inside out and made a crust out of potato and the filling out of peas and spices.

CALORIES	97 calories
FAT	2.2 grams
PROTEIN	3.8 grams
SODIUM	74 mg
CARBOHYDRATES	15.5 grams
SUGARS	1.4 grams
FIBER	1.5 grams

stuffed gnocchi

Makes 9

 Regular

16 ounces frozen gnocchi, thawed

2 tablespoons olive oil

¼ teaspoon salt, plus ⅛ teaspoon for filling

⅛ teaspoon pepper, plus ⅛ teaspoon for filling

1 cup frozen peas, thawed

1 scallion, chopped

2 tablespoons heavy cream

2 tablespoons chopped cooked pancetta

¼ cup frozen chopped spinach, thawed and squeezed dry

¼ cup grated Parmesan or Romano cheese

1 clove garlic, chopped finely

1. Preheat oven to 400°F and prepare 9 regular muffin cups by spraying with cooking spray.

2. Place gnocchi, olive oil, salt and pepper in the food processor, and process until it resembles coarse meal.

3. Divide dough among muffin cups and press into the bottoms and sides.

4. Spray the insides with cooking spray and bake for about 17 minutes, until solid and crispy.

5. Mix peas, scallion, cream, pancetta, salt, pepper, spinach, cheese, and garlic in a bowl until combined. Divide among the cups.

6. Bake for 10 minutes until filling is heated through.

You could fill these delicious cups with just about anything you wanted, like sausage or chicken, for different flavors.

CALORIES	152 calories
FAT	6.6 grams
PROTEIN	4.4 grams
SODIUM	501 mg
CARBOHYDRATES	18.4 grams
SUGARS	0.8 gram
FIBER	2.3 grams

baked angel hair with fresh herbs

Makes 12

Regular

3 cups cooked angel hair pasta, cut into 1" pieces
½ cup part-skim ricotta cheese
2 egg whites
¼ teaspoon salt
⅛ teaspoon pepper
1 tablespoon olive oil
¼ cup fresh mixed herbs (such as chives, oregano, basil, thyme, and rosemary)
2 tablespoons chopped cooked pancetta
¼ teaspoon ground red pepper

1. Preheat oven to 400°F and prepare 12 regular muffin cups with silicone liners.

2. Mix all ingredients together in a bowl, then divide among cups.

3. Bake for 10 minutes, then broil for 2 until golden.

Fresh herbs are the key to this recipe, making the dish bright, colorful, and full of vibrant flavor. Mix and match your favorites to vary the taste.

CALORIES	90 calories
FAT	3 grams
PROTEIN	4.1 grams
SODIUM	96 mg
CARBOHYDRATES	11.5 grams
SUGARS	0.3 gram
FIBER	0.6 gram

italian mac and cheese

Makes 9

 Regular

¼ small onion, chopped
1 tablespoon butter
12 cherry tomatoes, halved
1 small garlic clove
2 tablespoons Wondra flour
1 cup skim milk
⅓ cup shredded Romano cheese
⅓ cup shredded Asiago cheese
⅓ cup shredded Parmesan
   cheese
¼ cup shredded part-skim mozzarella, plus additional ⅓ cup
   for topping
1 tablespoon packed fresh
   chopped basil
1 tablespoon packed fresh
   chopped parsley
Salt and pepper to taste
1 cup elbow macaroni, cooked
   according to package
   instructions

1. Preheat oven to 400°F and prepare 9 regular muffin cups with silicone or foil liners.

2. In a skillet over medium-high heat, cook onion, butter, and tomatoes, until the onion is soft and tomatoes begin to fall apart.

3. Reduce heat to medium and stir in garlic and cook for 1 minute.

4. Stir in Wondra and cook for one minute.

5. Stir in milk and cook until thickened, 2–3 minutes.

6. Stir in cheeses, basil, parsley, and salt and pepper, and cook until the cheeses have melted. Add macaroni.

7. Divide among cups and top with remaining mozzarella.

8. Bake for 10 minutes, then broil for about 2 until tops are golden.

Enjoy mac and cheese taken to a new level. Add ¼ cup chopped pepperoni or cooked Italian sausage for additional flavor.

CALORIES	119 calories
FAT	5.4 grams
PROTEIN	7.5 grams
SODIUM	212 mg
CARBOHYDRATES	9.4 grams
SUGARS	2.3 grams
FIBER	0.8 gram

shrimp risotto

Makes 6

 Jumbo

1 cup Arborio rice
1 tablespoon olive oil
¼ teaspoon onion powder
Salt and pepper, to taste
12 raw, peeled shrimp
½ cup frozen peas (thawed)
2 cups low-sodium chicken stock
¼ cup chopped parsley
½ cup grated Parmesan cheese,
    plus ¼ cup reserved

1. Preheat oven to 300°F.

2. Prepare 6 jumbo muffin cups by spraying with cooking spray or lining with foil or silicone liners.

3. Mix rice, oil, onion powder, and salt and pepper in a bowl and allow it to rest about 15 minutes.

4. Mix in the rest of the ingredients.

5. Distribute among the cups, making sure there are 2 shrimp per cup and top with reserved cheese.

6. Bake for 30 minutes until shrimp is cooked through.

This no-fuss method creates a simplified risotto without all the stirring. Enjoy with Savory Carrot "Cakes" (see Chapter 7).

CALORIES	130 calories
FAT	5.7 grams
PROTEIN	9 grams
SODIUM	469 mg
CARBOHYDRATES	10.3 grams
SUGARS	1 gram
FIBER	0.8 gram

Chapter 7

Vegetables

Muffin tin cooking is a great alternative to steaming or boiling your veggies. When your vegetables become interesting and creative, you're more likely to eat them (and so are your kids!), so explore the great ideas in this chapter. When you bake vegetables in the oven, the natural sweetness becomes more accentuated, giving more flavor to your dishes.

lucky bamboo asparagus

Makes 10–12

Mini

2 bunches asparagus, ends trimmed
4 tablespoons lemon olive oil
2 tablespoons balsamic vinegar
Salt and pepper

1. Preheat oven to 350°F.

2. Spray 12 mini muffin cups with cooking spray.

3. Cut the asparagus into 2½–3" long pieces.

4. Cut 10–12 pieces of kitchen twine into 10" pieces. You can also use strips of 1" wide cheesecloth.

5. Stand asparagus up in each mini muffin cup until the cup is full (depending on the size of your asparagus, you will fill 10–12 cups), then tie the asparagus with the twine or cheesecloth, making a double knot.

6. Cut off the ends of the twine or cheesecloth.

7. Drizzle 1 teaspoon oil and ½ teaspoon vinegar on each asparagus package and season with salt and pepper.

8. Bake for 20 minutes, until asparagus is tender.

Serve the packages standing up, but be sure your diners remove the twine or string before eating. Lemon olive oil is olive oil infused with lemon flavor. You can substitute regular olive oil with a small amount of lemon juice if you can't find it.

CALORIES	48 calories
FAT	4.4 grams
PROTEIN	0.7 gram
SODIUM	13 mg
CARBOHYDRATES	1.7 grams
SUGARS	1 gram
FIBER	0.7 gram

zucchini, corn, and tomato cups

Makes 12

 Regular

1 cup fresh corn, cut off the cob (substitute frozen if not available)

1 cup zucchini, sliced thin and quartered

1 cup diced fresh tomato

4 teaspoons olive oil

¼ teaspoon garlic powder

½ teaspoon chopped fresh cilantro

Salt and pepper to taste

1. Preheat oven to 350°F.

2. Line a regular muffin tin with 12 foil or silicone liners. Mix all ingredients in a bowl, then portion the mixture out into the cups, filling all the way to the top.

3. Bake for 15 minutes until vegetables are cooked through.

This is the perfect dish to make when faced with the summer bounty of vegetables from your garden, the farmers' market, or supermarket. You can use yellow squash instead of zucchini, but your dish won't be as colorful.

CALORIES	33 calories
FAT	1.6 grams
PROTEIN	0.7 gram
SODIUM	14 mg
CARBOHYDRATES	4 grams
SUGARS	1.2 grams
FIBER	0.7 gram

squash casserole

Makes 6

 Regular

1 tablespoon olive oil
1 small yellow squash, thinly sliced, then cut in half
1 small zucchini, thinly sliced, then cut in half
½ small onion, thinly sliced
½ large tomato, or 1 medium, thinly sliced
¼ teaspoon dried thyme
Salt and pepper
¼ cup chicken broth
2 teaspoons cornstarch
1 ounce goat cheese
½ tablespoon seasoned bread crumbs
1 tablespoon shredded part-skim mozzarella cheese

1. Preheat oven to 350°F, and prepare 6 regular muffin cups with foil or silicone liners.

2. In a sauté pan, heat olive oil over medium-high heat and add squashes, onion, and tomato. Cook, stirring, until vegetables soften.

3. Add thyme, salt, pepper, broth, and cornstarch, and cook until thickened, 1–2 minutes.

4. Add goat cheese and stir until melted and combined.

5. Divide among muffin tins and top with bread crumbs and mozzarella.

6. Bake for 10 minutes until squash is cooked through.

Use any cheese you like in this recipe, and feel free to use all zucchini or all yellow squash if you have some to use up.

CALORIES	68 calories
FAT	4.1 grams
PROTEIN	2.8 grams
SODIUM	93 mg
CARBOHYDRATES	4.9 grams
SUGARS	2.4 grams
FIBER	1 gram

french onion pie

Makes 6

1 unbaked refrigerated pie crust
2 large sweet onions, peeled
   and thinly sliced
1 tablespoon olive oil
1 tablespoon unsalted butter
½ teaspoon salt
½ teaspoon sugar
2 tablespoons Wondra flour
1 tablespoon sherry
1 cup beef broth
Pepper
⅓ cup grated Swiss cheese, plus
   2 tablespoons for topping

1. Preheat oven to 350°F, and prepare 6 regular muffin cups.

2. Follow the instructions in "Using Pie Crusts" in the Introduction to prepare the pie crust.

3. Place a large skillet over medium heat, and add onions, olive oil, and butter.

4. Cook, stirring occasionally for about ½ an hour until onions are caramelized.

5. Add salt and sugar and reduce heat to medium-low and continue cooking and stirring about ½ an hour, until the onions are a deep golden color.

6. Stir in flour and cook about 1 minute.

7. Stir in sherry and cook until it evaporates, about 1 minute.

8. Stir in beef broth and add pepper, cooking until mixture becomes very thick, about 4–5 minutes.

9. Stir in cheese until it is combined and melted.

10. Fill cups with onion mixture, topping with reserved cheese.

11. Bake 25 minutes until pie crust is golden.

I've fallen hard for this dish and may never go back to the traditional soup. Each pie is packed with creamy, golden caramelized onions that are delicious and sweet.

CALORIES	224 calories
FAT	13.8 grams
PROTEIN	3.6 grams
SODIUM	530 mg
CARBOHYDRATES	22.1 grams
SUGARS	2 grams
FIBER	0.7 gram

edamame in rice paper cups

Makes 4

 Jumbo

4 round rice paper wrappers
1 10-ounce package edamame beans, shelled
1 teaspoon sesame oil
½ teaspoon fresh grated gingerroot
Salt and pepper

1. Preheat oven to 400°F and prepare 4 jumbo muffin cups by spraying with cooking spray.

2. Soak rice paper wrappers in warm water until pliable.

3. Place 1 wrapper in each cup, pressing down to conform to the shape of the cup.

4. Mix edamame, oil, ginger, salt and pepper in a bowl and divide among the cups.

5. Bake for 8 minutes until cooked through.

CALORIES	98 calories
FAT	1.2 grams
PROTEIN	8.1 grams
SODIUM	40 mg
CARBOHYDRATES	13.7 grams
SUGARS	1.8 grams
FIBER	3.4 grams

cauliflower gratin

Makes 4

 Jumbo

2 cups roughly chopped cauliflower
½ cup seasoned bread crumbs
Salt and pepper to taste
2 tablespoons melted unsalted butter
¼ cup grated Gruyère cheese
½ cup skim milk
1 tablespoon olive oil
Pinch of nutmeg

1. Preheat oven to 400°F and prepare 4 jumbo muffin cups with foil or silicone liners.

2. Place all ingredients in a bowl and toss to mix.

3. Divide among muffin cups.

4. Bake for 30 minutes, until bubbly and brown.

Cauliflower is dressed up as a gratin and feels oh-so-sophisticated in this dish.

CALORIES	187 calories
FAT	11.6 grams
PROTEIN	6.3 grams
SODIUM	355 mg
CARBOHYDRATES	14.5 grams
SUGARS	3.5 grams
FIBER	1.8 grams

cherry tomato cups

Makes 4

 Regular

1 cup cherry tomatoes
1 tablespoon olive oil
Salt and pepper to taste
½ teaspoon Italian seasoning
⅛ teaspoon garlic powder
1 teaspoon seasoned bread crumbs
1 tablespoon shredded part-skim mozzarella cheese

1. Preheat oven to 400°F and prepare 4 regular muffin cups with silicone or foil liners.

2. Mix all ingredients, then divide among cups.

3. Bake for 25 minutes, until tomatoes wrinkle and begin to split.

This is fast and easy to make and is a colorful side dish that pairs well with Chicken with Caper and Dill Sauce (see Chapter 4).

CALORIES	43 calories
FAT	3.7 grams
PROTEIN	0.9 gram
SODIUM	60 mg
CARBOHYDRATES	1.9 grams
SUGARS	1 gram
FIBER	0.5 gram

roasted swiss chard

Makes 4

Jumbo

1 bunch Swiss chard, roughly chopped
1 tablespoon olive oil
1 tablespoon balsamic vinegar
⅛ teaspoon salt
⅛ teaspoon pepper

1. Preheat oven to 400°F and prepare 4 jumbo muffin cups with silicone liners.

2. Toss all ingredients together in a bowl, then divide among cups.

3. Bake for about 25 minutes, stirring halfway through, until Swiss chard is cooked through.

The Swiss chard stems remain slightly crunchy, which allows for a nice contrast in texture. Use any color Swiss chard you like.

CALORIES	40 calories
FAT	3.3 grams
PROTEIN	0.7 gram
SODIUM	149 mg
CARBOHYDRATES	2 grams
SUGARS	1 gram
FIBER	0.6 gram

cheesy asparagus

Maker 12

 Regular

24 stalks asparagus, ends
   trimmed
½ cup seasoned bread crumbs
½ cup fontinella cheese, grated
Salt and pepper
2 teaspoons dry mustard
6 tablespoons heavy cream
6 tablespoons skim milk

1. Preheat oven to 400°F.

2. Prepare 12 regular muffin cups with foil or silicone liners.

3. Cut asparagus into 1½" pieces and divide among the cups.

4. Sprinkle the cups with the bread crumbs, then the cheese.

5. Mix remaining ingredients in a small bowl.

6. Place about 1 tablespoon of the mixture in each cup.

7. Bake for 18 minutes until asparagus is cooked through.

Serve with Tilapia Florentine (see Chapter 5) and Tea Muffins with Flavored Butter (see Chapter 8) for a tasty dinner.

CALORIES	71 calories
FAT	4.25 grams
PROTEIN	3 grams
SODIUM	143 mg
CARBOHYDRATES	5.3 grams
SUGARS	1.4 grams
FIBER	0.9 gram

minestrone pie

Makes 6

 Jumbo

2 unbaked refrigerated pie crusts
½ small onion, chopped
1 tablespoon olive oil
1 cup chopped zucchini
Salt and pepper to taste
1 tablespoon Italian seasoning
1 cup frozen mixed vegetables, thawed
½ cup canned light or dark kidney beans, drained
2 tablespoons Wondra flour
½ cup beef broth
1 beef bouillon cube
¾ of a 14.5-ounce can of diced tomatoes, with juice
6 tablespoons Romano cheese

1. Preheat oven to 400°F and prepare 6 jumbo muffin cups with silicone liners.

2. Follow the instructions in the Introduction in "Using Pie Crusts" but use two crusts and cut out 6 5" circles.

3. Add salt, pepper, Italian seasoning, mixed vegetables, and beans, and cook until hot.

4. Stir in Wondra and cook for about 30 seconds, then add beef broth, bouillon, and tomatoes. Stir until thickened.

5. Divide among cups and top with 1 tablespoon cheese on each.

6. Bake for about 17–20 minutes until bubbling and crust is golden.

Another soup-in-a-mini-pie (see also French Onion Pie, earlier in this chapter), this dish is filled with hearty vegetables and brings lots of variety to the table.

CALORIES	315 calories
FAT	16.3 grams
PROTEIN	9.3 grams
SODIUM	731 mg
CARBOHYDRATES	35.3 grams
SUGARS	2.8 grams
FIBER	4 grams

zesty corn cups

Makes 6

 Regular

3 tablespoons unsalted butter
2 wedges Laughing Cow Light Queso Fresco & Chipotle cheese
3 ears corn on the cob, kernels cut off (or about 2¼ cups frozen corn)
Salt and pepper to taste
1 tablespoon chopped fresh cilantro
1 tablespoon skim milk

1. Preheat oven to 400°F and prepare 6 cups in a regular muffin tin with foil or silicone liners.

2. Melt butter and cheese in a small bowl in the microwave.

3. Mix butter and cheese with other ingredients in a bowl.

4. Divide among the cups.

5. Bake for 17 minutes until corn is cooked through.

This is a takeoff on Mexican corn on the cob, where the cobs are rubbed with butter and cheese and sprinkled with herbs.

CALORIES	125 calories
FAT	6.3 grams
PROTEIN	2.7 grams
SODIUM	108 mg
CARBOHYDRATES	14.6 grams
SUGARS	2.7 grams
FIBER	1.7 grams

tomato pie

Makes 4

 Jumbo

4 teaspoons seasoned bread crumbs, plus 1 tablespoon for topping

2 or 3 ripe tomatoes, about the diameter of a jumbo muffin cup, sliced about ¼" thick, for a total of 16 slices

1 scallion, chopped

Italian herb mix to taste

Salt and pepper to taste

2 slices Swiss cheese, chopped, with about 16 chopped pieces reserved

2 eggs

1 tablespoon cream

1. Preheat oven to 325°F and line 4 jumbo muffin cups with foil or silicone liners.

2. Spray the inside of the liners with cooking spray, then sprinkle 1 teaspoon of bread crumbs in each, shaking to coat the sides and bottom as best you can.

3. Make 3 layers in each cup. Make each layer by starting with a tomato slice, then adding a bit of scallion, a pinch of Italian herb mix, a dash of salt and pepper, and some cheese. After the three layers, finish by topping with a tomato slice.

4. Mix eggs and cream well, and divide among the cups, pouring ¼ of the mixture in each cup over the tomatoes (this will not completely fill the cups).

5. Divide remaining 1 tablespoon bread crumbs among the cups, and top with the remaining cheese.

6. Spray the tops with cooking spray, then bake for 40 minutes until the egg is set, the tomatoes are cooked and the top is golden.

I make this often in late summer, when I have lots of big, ripe tomatoes on hand. If you have some fresh basil and oregano, chop about 1 tablespoon of each and use that in place of the dried Italian herb mix. You can also just layer in 1 basil leaf in each layer you make. Another variation is to add some crumbled bacon.

CALORIES	135 calories
FAT	7.5 grams
PROTEIN	8.5 grams
SODIUM	181 mg
CARBOHYDRATES	7.9 grams
SUGARS	3.1 grams
FIBER	1.4 grams

corn pudding

Makes 9

 Regular

1 8.5-ounce can creamed corn
1 egg
½ teaspoon salt
½ teaspoon sugar
⅛ teaspoon pepper
¼ cup flour
1 tablespoon melted unsalted
   butter
½ cup skim milk
½ cup heavy cream
⅛ teaspoon chopped red bell
   pepper
½ shallot, chopped

1. Preheat oven to 325°F and prepare 9 regular muffin cups with silicone liners.

2. Whisk all ingredients together well and divide among cups.

3. Place ½" hot water in a roasting pan and set the muffin pan in in it.

4. Bake for 1 hour, or until custard is completely set.

The easiest way to manage all the components to this dish is to place the muffin tin in your roasting pan on the oven rack, then slowly pour your hot water into the pan. This way you will avoid sloshing water into the puddings.

CALORIES	105 calories
FAT	6.3 grams
PROTEIN	2.2 grams
SODIUM	241 mg
CARBOHYDRATES	8.9 grams
SUGARS	2 grams
FIBER	0.9 gram

spinach cakes

Makes 20 mini or 7 regular

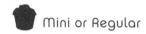 Mini or Regular

10 ounces frozen chopped spinach, defrosted and squeezed dry

1 egg

¼ cup plus 2 tablespoons seasoned bread crumbs

Salt and pepper to taste

2 ounces goat cheese

¼ teaspoon dried oregano

1 tablespoon olive oil

1 tablespoon heavy cream

1 garlic clove, minced

⅓ medium zucchini, chopped

¼ medium onion, chopped

1. Preheat oven to 400°F.

2. Prepare either mini or regular cups by spraying with cooking spray.

3. Mix all ingredients together well.

4. Divide among the cups and bake for 12 minutes for mini muffin cups or 18 minutes for regular until slightly browned.

Make this in mini muffin cups for an appetizer. An easy way to make this recipe without a lot of chopping is to place all ingredients, including the unchopped onion, garlic, and zucchini, in a food processor and process until combined.

CALORIES	105 calories/ 37 calories (7 full servings/ 20 mini servings)
FAT	5.9 grams/ 2.1 grams
PROTEIN	5.4 grams/ 1.9 grams
SODIUM	317 mg/ 111 mg
CARBOHYDRATES	7.5 grams/ 2.6 grams
SUGARS	1.2 grams/ 0.4 gram
FIBER	2 grams/ 0.7 gram

broccoli soufflé cups

Makes 8

 Jumbo

1 cup skim milk
¼ cup unsalted butter
¼ teaspoon salt
⅛ teaspoon pepper
¼ teaspoon dry mustard
¼ cup flour
1 cup shredded sharp cheddar
   cheese
¾ cup cooked, chopped
   broccoli
3 eggs, separated
¼ teaspoon cream of tartar

1. Preheat oven to 350°F.

2. Prepare 8 jumbo muffin cups with silicone liners.

3. Place milk and butter in a saucepan over medium heat. Stir until butter has melted.

4. Stir in salt, pepper, dry mustard, and flour and cook until sauce is thickened.

5. Stir in cheese, until melted, then stir in broccoli.

6. Stir in egg yolks, one at a time.

7. In a bowl, beat the egg whites with cream of tartar until stiff peaks form.

8. Carefully fold the egg whites into the broccoli mixture.

9. Divide mixture among the muffin cups. Using a knife, make a circle in the batter, about ½" in from the rim of each soufflé.

10. Place the muffin tin in a roasting pan in the oven, then add 1" hot water to the roasting pan.

11. Bake for 30 minutes, until the soufflés are puffed. Carefully remove the cups from the pan and serve immediately.

You can use foil muffin cup liners for this, but they do not perform as well as the silicone liners. Do not make this in a muffin tin without liners, because you cannot remove the soufflés without them deflating. See the sidebar for Corn Pudding in this chapter for tips on how to manage roasting pan, water, and muffin tins easily.

CALORIES	160 calories
FAT	11.6 grams
PROTEIN	7.8 grams
SODIUM	209 mg
CARBOHYDRATES	6 grams
SUGARS	1.9 grams
FIBER	0.6 gram

brussels sprouts cups

Makes 12

 Regular

1 pound Brussels sprouts,
   trimmed and cut into quarters
1 tablespoon olive oil
1 tablespoon melted unsalted
   butter
¼ cup plus 1 tablespoon
   chopped pecans
⅛ teaspoon onion powder
1 tablespoon brown sugar
Salt and pepper, to taste
Pinch of nutmeg

1. Preheat oven to 400°F and prepare 12 regular muffin cups with foil or silicone liners.

2. Mix all ingredients in a bowl, tossing to combine.

3. Divide among muffin cups and bake for 25 minutes until the sprouts are tender.

Brussels sprouts develop a slightly sweet taste when they are roasted, and this is deepened by the other ingredients in this dish.

CALORIES	60 calories
FAT	4 grams
PROTEIN	1.6 grams
SODIUM	21 mg
CARBOHYDRATES	4.9 grams
SUGARS	2.1 grams
FIBER	1.7 grams

mushroom tarts

Makes 8

 Regular

1 tube of 8 refrigerated crescent roll dough
1 small shallot, chopped
1 tablespoon olive oil
5 ounces baby bella or white mushrooms, sliced
4 ounces shiitake mushrooms, sliced, stems removed
Salt and pepper
1 tablespoon sherry
⅛ teaspoon dry mustard
Pinch thyme
1 tablespoon fresh chopped parsley
¼ cup extra sharp shredded provolone cheese

1. Preheat oven to 400°F.

2. Prepare 8 regular muffin cups.

3. Follow instructions on "Crescent Dough Crusts" in the Introduction to prepare crescent roll dough. Place in cups.

4. In a skillet over medium heat, cook shallot in oil, until translucent. Add mushrooms, cooking until completely cooked and soft.

5. Stir in salt, pepper, sherry, dry mustard, thyme, and parsley, and cook until sherry has evaporated, 1–2 minutes.

6. Turn off heat, and stir in cheese.

7. Divide mushroom mixture among the cups and bake for 10 minutes, until crescent dough is golden.

Use fresh shiitake mushrooms. Shiitakes are a mushroom often used in Asian cooking and are sometimes sold dried, but dried mushrooms do not work well in this recipe.

CALORIES	139 calories
FAT	8.7 grams
PROTEIN	3.9 grams
SODIUM	276 mg
CARBOHYDRATES	12.7 grams
SUGARS	3.7 grams
FIBER	0.5 gram

savory carrot "cakes"

Makes 12

 Mini

8 ounces baby carrots
¼ large shallot, peeled
1 tablespoon olive oil
½ teaspoon grated fresh
    gingerroot
Salt and pepper to taste
2 tablespoons orange juice
2 ounces light cream cheese
¼ cup panko

1. Preheat oven to 400°F and prepare 12 mini muffin cups by spraying with cooking spray.

2. Place carrots and shallot in the food processor and pulse until finely chopped.

3. Put olive oil in a sauté pan and add carrot-shallot mix.

4. Add ginger, salt, pepper, and orange juice.

5. Cook over medium-high heat until vegetables are softened.

6. Turn off the heat and stir in cream cheese until completely melted and combined, then stir in panko.

7. Divide among the cups and bake for 15 minutes until slightly browned at the edges and set in the middle.

Panko is Japanese-style bread crumbs and can often be found gluten-free. Not all panko is gluten-free though, so be sure to check the labels if this is a requirement for you.

CALORIES	32 calories
FAT	1.8 grams
PROTEIN	0.6 gram
SODIUM	52 mg
CARBOHYDRATES	2.7 grams
SUGARS	1.4 grams
FIBER	0.6 gram

smashed pea cups

Makes 9

Regular

1½ cups cooked peas, plus ½
    cup reserved
2 tablespoons cream
Salt and pepper
1 tablespoon unsalted butter
2 slices deli ham, chopped
Green part of 1 scallion,
    chopped
1 teaspoon cornstarch
3 tablespoons Parmesan cheese

1. Preheat oven to 400°F and prepare 9 regular muffin cups with silicone or foil liners.

2. Place hot peas in a bowl and smash them.

3. Mix in cream, salt, pepper, and butter.

4. Stir in reserved peas, ham, scallion, and cornstarch.

5. Divide among muffin cups and top with Parmesan cheese.

6. Bake for 15 minutes until heated through and slightly set.

This is my take on British mushy peas, and is definitely more flavorful and has lots more texture than the original dish.

CALORIES	69 calories
FAT	3.4 grams
PROTEIN	3.6 grams
SODIUM	149 mg
CARBOHYDRATES	5.9 grams
SUGARS	1.7 grams
FIBER	2.1 grams

baked veggie stir-fry

Makes 9

Regular

Green part of 1 scallion, chopped
8 baby carrots, cut into thin rounds
2 cups broccoli florets
1 cup bean sprouts
1 small garlic clove, chopped
¼ cup bottled stir-fry sauce
1 teaspoon tamari sauce
1 tablespoon olive oil

1. Preheat oven to 400°F and prepare 9 regular muffin cups with foil or silicone liners

2. Place all ingredients in a bowl and toss to coat.

3. Divide among the cups, scraping bowl with a rubber scraper to get all the sauce.

4. Bake for 20 minutes until vegetables are cooked.

Enjoy your stir-fry without all the stirring when you make it in muffin cups. The beauty of stir-fry is that you can throw in any vegetables you happen to have hanging around. Try it with snow peas, cauliflower, bok choy—anything!

CALORIES	41 calories
FAT	1.6 grams
PROTEIN	1.3 grams
SODIUM	290 mg
CARBOHYDRATES	5.9 grams
SUGARS	2.7 grams
FIBER	1.6 grams

stewed tomato cups

Makes 8

 Regular

2 teaspoons brown sugar
4 teaspoons Wondra flour
1 teaspoon salt
⅛ teaspoon onion powder
4 medium tomatoes, peeled (see sidebar), seeded, chopped
4 tablespoons melted unsalted butter
¼ teaspoon ground pepper
2 fresh basil leaves, chopped, plus 8 whole small leaves reserved for garnish

1. Preheat the oven to 400°F and prepare 8 regular muffin cups with silicone liners.

2. Mix all ingredients in a bowl.

3. Divide among muffin cups and bake for 27–30 minutes, until bubbling.

4. Garnish each with a small basil leaf before serving.

To easily peel tomatoes, drop them into a pot of boiling water for about 30 seconds. Allow to cool, and the skins will slip right off.

CALORIES	70 calories
FAT	5.4 grams
PROTEIN	0.7 gram
SODIUM	294 mg
CARBOHYDRATES	4.5 grams
SUGARS	2.7 grams
FIBER	0.8 gram

baked bean pies with slaw

Makes 10

Regular

3 slices prosciutto
2 unbaked refrigerated pie crusts
1 can baked beans (1 pound, 4 ounces)
¼ cup ketchup
1 teaspoon cider vinegar
1 teaspoon Worcestershire sauce
1 teaspoon yellow mustard
1 tablespoon brown sugar

For slaw:
4 cups shredded cabbage slaw
½ cup light mayonnaise
3 teaspoons sugar
2 tablespoons heavy cream
2 teaspoons cider vinegar

1. Preheat oven to 400°F.

2. Place prosciutto slices on a greased baking sheet and bake for about 8 minutes, until crisp.

3. Prepare 10 regular muffin cups.

4. Follow the instructions in "Using Pie Crusts" in the Introduction to prepare the pie crust dough. Make 10 pie crusts and place in cups.

5. Mix baked beans, ketchup, vinegar, Worcestershire, mustard, and brown sugar in a bowl.

6. Crumble in the prosciutto and mix.

7. Divide among muffin cups and bake 20–25 minutes until bubbly.

8. To make the slaw, place the cabbage, mayonnaise, sugar, cream, and cider vinegar in a bowl. Mix. Refrigerate until ready to serve.

9. Top each pie with slaw before serving.

Serve these for a summer supper and your dinner guests will be wowed by how pretty they are. You can use any kind of slaw you like for this recipe, but I like to buy packaged rainbow slaw, which includes broccoli and carrots.

CALORIES	290 calories
FAT	14.1 grams
PROTEIN	6.1 grams
SODIUM	715 mg
CARBOHYDRATES	35 grams
SUGARS	9.9 grams
FIBER	3.1 grams

green beans and mushrooms

Makes 6

1 cup green beans, trimmed and cut into 1" pieces
½ cup sliced mushrooms
1 tablespoon basting oil (see sidebar)
Salt and pepper
½ teaspoon Worcestershire sauce

1. Preheat oven to 400°F and prepare 6 regular muffin cups by lining with foil or silicone liners.

2. Toss beans, mushrooms, oil, salt, pepper and Worcestershire sauce in a bowl, then divide among the cups.

3. Bake for 25 minutes until beans are tender.

Basting oil is oil flavored with herbs and seasonings. You can make your own by mixing 1 cup of olive oil with 2 teaspoons of any dried herbs and allowing it to soak for a few hours, so the flavors infuse.

CALORIES	26 calories
FAT	2.2 grams
PROTEIN	0.5 gram
SODIUM	30 mg
CARBOHYDRATES	1.4 grams
SUGARS	0.7 gram
FIBER	0.5 gram

Chapter 8

Muffins and Breads

You're likely expecting muffin recipes in a muffin tin cookbook. And you're right! You'll find plenty of muffin recipes in this chapter. But you also find scones, breads, and biscuit recipes that you can make in your muffin tin. You'll find some recipes in this chapter that everyone should have as standbys, but you'll also come across some fun, new ideas and flavors.

corn muffins

Makes 12

Regular

1 cup whole wheat pastry flour
1 cup stone-ground cornmeal
2 eggs
1¼ cups buttermilk
3 tablespoons unsalted butter, melted
¼ cup honey
4 teaspoons baking powder
¼ teaspoon salt

1. Preheat oven to 425°F.

2. Prepare 12 regular muffin cups by spraying or lining with liners.

3. Combine all of the ingredients in a bowl, until completely mixed.

4. Divide the batter among the cups.

5. Bake for 10–12 minutes, until a cake tester comes out clean.

I buy my cornmeal from the Jenney Grist Mill (*www.jenneygristmill.org*) in Plymouth, Massachusetts, where you can watch an historic grist mill in action and buy freshly ground cornmeal (so fresh, you must keep it in the freezer). It has a very different taste from traditional store-bought cornmeal.

CALORIES	147 calories
FAT	4.3 grams
PROTEIN	4 grams
SODIUM	248 mg
CARBOHYDRATES	22.8 grams
SUGARS	7.25 grams
FIBER	1.8 grams

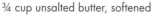

banana pecan muffins

Makes 12

 Regular

¾ cup unsalted butter, softened
1 cup sugar
3 overripe bananas, removed
    from skins
1 egg
1 cup white flour
1 cup whole wheat pastry flour
1½ teaspoons baking powder
¼ teaspoon salt
½ teaspoon cinnamon
2 teaspoons ground flaxseed
½ cup chopped pecans
Cinnamon sugar, for topping

1. Preheat the oven to 350°F.

2. Prepare 12 regular muffin cups with cooking spray or liners.

3. Beat butter and sugar until combined.

4. Add bananas and beat until combined. Add egg and combine.

5. Add both flours, baking powder, salt, cinnamon, and flaxseed and beat until combined.

6. Fold in pecans.

7. Fill muffin cups almost to the top.

8. Sprinkle the tops with cinnamon sugar.

9. Bake for 25–30 minutes, until a cake tester comes out clean.

To easily fill muffin cups with batter, use an ice cream scoop (the kind with the handle you squeeze that has a bar that swipes across the inside of the cup). It is the perfect size and drops the batter out perfectly. Enjoy these with honey or Flavored Butter (see Tea Muffins with Flavored Butter, later in this chapter). You can make your own cinnamon sugar by mixing ¼ cup sugar with ¾ teaspoon cinnamon. Keep it in a shaker to use on toast, pudding, waffles and desserts.

CALORIES	307 calories
FAT	7.8 grams
PROTEIN	3.5 grams
SODIUM	117 mg
CARBOHYDRATES	39.7 grams
SUGARS	20.5 grams
FIBER	2.6 grams

monkey bread

Makes 8

 Regular

1 tube of regular-size biscuits (10 pieces)
⅓ cup sugar
¾ teaspoon cinnamon
3 tablespoons unsalted butter, melted

1. Preheat oven to 400°F and prepare 8 regular muffin cups by spraying with cooking spray or lining with foil or silicone liners.

2. Cut the biscuits into 4 pieces each and roll into balls.

3. Mix sugar and cinnamon in a small bowl.

4. Dip the balls in the melted butter, then the cinnamon sugar mixture, coating completely.

5. Place 5 balls in each cup (4 on the bottom and 1 on top).

6. Bake for 10–13 minutes (baking time will be closer to 10 minutes if you bake right in the cup, longer if you use liners).

This is a great dish for kids to make. You can also make your own biscuit dough and roll that into balls, then roll into cinnamon-sugar and bake. Use the recipe for Rosemary Biscuits (later in this chapter), and just omit the rosemary.

CALORIES	195 calories
FAT	7.7 grams
PROTEIN	2.5 grams
SODIUM	413 mg
CARBOHYDRATES	27.3 grams
SUGARS	12.1 grams
FIBER	0.8 gram

pizza muffins

Makes 12

 Regular

1½ cups flour
½ cup whole wheat pastry flour
2 teaspoons baking powder
1 teaspoon sugar
½ teaspoon salt
⅛ teaspoon ground pepper
¼ cup olive oil
1 egg
¾ cup tomato sauce
1 tablespoon tomato paste
½ teaspoon dried basil
½ teaspoon dried oregano
¼ teaspoon garlic powder
½ cup cubed part-skim mozza-
    rella (¼" cubes)
¼ cup shredded Parmesan
    cheese, plus more for topping
¼ cup chopped pepperoni

1. Preheat oven to 400°F and prepare 12 regular muffin cups by spraying with cooking spray.

2. Mix flours, baking powder, sugar, salt, and pepper in a bowl. Set aside.

3. In another bowl, mix oil, egg, tomato sauce, and tomato paste.

4. Add basil, oregano, garlic powder, mozzarella, Parmesan, and pepperoni to dry mixture, stirring.

5. Stir in wet ingredients until combined.

6. Divide among cups and sprinkle the tops with Parmesan cheese.

7. Bake for 14 minutes until a cake tester comes out clean.

Turkey pepperoni is a lower-calorie substitution you can make in this recipe. These muffins are great to pack in lunches, as they are very filling.

CALORIES	170 calories
FAT	7.4 grams
PROTEIN	6 grams
SODIUM	323 mg
CARBOHYDRATES	19.6 grams
SUGARS	2.5 grams
FIBER	1.6 grams

blueberry streusel muffins

Makes 12

 Regular

1 egg
½ cup skim milk
¼ cup vegetable oil
¾ cup flour
¾ cup whole wheat pastry flour
½ cup sugar
2 teaspoons baking powder
½ teaspoon salt
1 cup fresh blueberries
½ teaspoon cinnamon
¾ cup Crumb Topping (from Nectarine Crisp with Crumb Topping, in Chapter 9)

1. Preheat oven to 400°F and prepare 12 regular muffin cups by spraying them with cooking spray.

2. Mix egg, milk, oil, flours, sugar, baking powder, and salt in a bowl.

3. Stir in blueberries and cinnamon.

4. Divide the batter among the muffin cups.

5. Top with crumb topping (about 1 tablespoon on each muffin).

6. Bake 20–25 minutes, until a cake tester comes out clean.

This is probably my all-time favorite muffin. These freeze well in a large plastic container. Frozen blueberries can be used in place of fresh in winter.

CALORIES	199 calories
FAT	7.3 grams
PROTEIN	2.8 grams
SODIUM	198 mg
CARBOHYDRATES	30.1 grams
SUGARS	15.5 grams
FIBER	1.6 grams

mini grilled cheese and tomato sandwiches

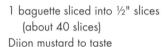Makes 20

 Regular

1 baguette sliced into ½" slices (about 40 slices)
Dijon mustard to taste
4 plum tomatoes, seeded and sliced thinly into 20 slices
10 slices of Swiss cheese, cut in half

1. Preheat oven to 400°F and prepare 20 regular muffin cups by spraying with cooking spray.

2. Spread mustard on one side of each slice of bread and pair them up so you have 20 pairs.

3. Place the tomato slices on paper towels to dry them, then place 1 on each sandwich.

4. For each sandwich, take ½ piece of Swiss cheese and fold in half, then place on top of tomato. Top with remaining piece of bread.

5. Place 1 sandwich in each muffin cup and spray the tops of the sandwiches with cooking spray.

6. Bake for about 5 minutes, until the cheese just melts and the tops of the sandwiches are golden brown.

This recipe is perfect for customizing, so try making it with ham added to each sandwich or with a different type of cheese. You can easily make up tons of these if you're feeding a large number of people.

CALORIES	137 calories
FAT	4.1 grams
PROTEIN	7.2 grams
SODIUM	172 mg
CARBOHYDRATES	17.2 grams
SUGARS	1.2 grams
FIBER	0.8 gram

peanut butter and jelly muffins

Makes 9

 Regular

¼ cup sugar
½ cup crunchy peanut butter
1 egg
¼ cup buttermilk
1 tablespoon light cream cheese
¼ cup skim milk
1½ cups flour
1 teaspoon baking powder
¼ teaspoon salt
½ cup chopped peanuts, plus
   whole peanuts for topping
3 tablespoons jelly or jam (any
   type you prefer)

1. Preheat oven to 400°F and prepare 9 regular muffin cups by spraying with cooking spray.

2. Beat sugar and peanut butter until combined, then add egg, buttermilk, cream cheese and milk.

3. Beat in dry ingredients, then stir in peanuts.

4. Divide into 9 balls.

5. Use your thumb or finger to create a deep hole and place 1 teaspoon jelly in each hole.

6. Seal up the hole and place seam side up in the cups.

7. Lightly press 2–3 whole peanuts on top of each.

8. Bake for 12 minutes until a cake tester comes out clean.

I like to use grape jelly in these muffins, but other varieties will work well. Slightly underbake these, and you will get a very soft peanut-buttery texture in the center. To make these even healthier, look for trans-fat-free peanut butter; if you're concerned about your sodium intake, look for unsalted peanut butter.

CALORIES	275 calories
FAT	12.4 grams
PROTEIN	9.1 grams
SODIUM	292 mg
CARBOHYDRATES	32.2 grams
SUGARS	11.3 grams
FIBER	2.5 grams

rosemary biscuits

Makes 6

 Regular

2 cups flour
3 teaspoons baking powder
¼ teaspoon salt
5 tablespoons unsalted butter, frozen
2 teaspoons dried rosemary
⅔ cup buttermilk

1. Preheat oven to 450°F and prepare 6 regular muffin cups.

2. Place flour, baking powder, and salt in a bowl.

3. Use a cheese grater to grate the butter into the bowl.

4. Rub dry ingredients into butter with your fingers until combined.

5. Stir in rosemary and buttermilk, using your hands.

6. Divide among muffin cups.

7. Bake for 12 minutes until biscuit is completely set.

If you don't have time to freeze your butter, you can cut refrigerated butter into small cubes and use a pastry cutter to combine it with the dry ingredients.

CALORIES	253 calories
FAT	10 grams
PROTEIN	5.3 grams
SODIUM	365 mg
CARBOHYDRATES	33.9 grams
SUGARS	1.7 grams
FIBER	1 gram

savory spinach muffins

Maker 12

 Regular

1 egg
1¼ cups skim milk
⅓ cup olive oil
1 cup flour
1 cup whole wheat pastry flour
1 tablespoon sugar
1 tablespoon baking powder
1 teaspoon dried basil
1 teaspoon onion powder
¼ teaspoon garlic powder
½ teaspoon salt
½ teaspoon pepper
⅓ cup grated Parmesan cheese, plus 2 tablespoons for topping
5 ounces (½ a package) frozen spinach, defrosted and squeezed dry

1. Preheat oven to 400°F and prepare 12 regular muffin cups by spraying with cooking spray.

2. Mix egg, milk, and oil in a large bowl.

3. Add flours, sugar, baking powder, basil, onion powder, garlic powder, salt, pepper, and Parmesan cheese and stir until well combined.

4. Add spinach and stir until combined

5. Fill muffin cups about ¾ full and sprinkle the remaining 2 tablespoons cheese on top of the muffins.

6. Bake for 12 minutes until a cake tester comes out clean.

People aren't used to eating green muffins, but this one will surely delight when they experience the burst of delicious flavors contained inside.

CALORIES	167 calories
FAT	7.6 grams
PROTEIN	5.3 grams
SODIUM	331 mg
CARBOHYDRATES	18.7 grams
SUGARS	2.5 grams
FIBER	1.7 grams

kiwi muffins with glaze

Makes 12

 Regular

1½ cups flour
2 teaspoons baking powder
½ cup sugar
½ teaspoon salt
1 egg
¼ cup vegetable oil
½ cup skim milk
4 kiwis, peeled and thinly sliced,
    then quartered
⅛ teaspoon nutmeg

Glaze

1 cup powdered sugar
2 tablespoons plus 1 teaspoon
    milk

1. Preheat oven to 400°F and prepare 12 regular muffin cups by spraying with cooking spray.

2. Mix flour, baking powder, sugar, and salt together in a bowl. Then add egg, oil, and milk.

3. Stir in kiwis and nutmeg.

4. Divide among muffin cups, and bake for 12–15 minutes until cake tester comes out clean.

Glaze

1. Completely combine all ingredients in a bowl, then drizzle over the tops of the muffins. Serve.

Kiwis are an unusual fruit to add to muffins, but when you taste these you'll wonder why more people haven't tried it. Be sure your kiwis are nice and ripe (they will be slightly soft to the touch) for the best flavor.

CALORIES	154 calories
FAT	5.1 grams
PROTEIN	2.7 grams
SODIUM	190 mg
CARBOHYDRATES	24.3 grams
SUGARS	11 grams
FIBER	1.1 grams

individual cheddar chive soda breads

Makes 12

 Regular

1½ cups flour
½ cup whole wheat flour
1 teaspoon baking powder
½ teaspoon salt
1 cup shredded sharp cheddar
  cheese
¼ cup fresh chopped chives
1 cup buttermilk
3 tablespoons softened unsalted
  butter
2 ounces softened light cream
  cheese
2 eggs
1 tablespoon water

1. Preheat oven to 350°F and prepare 12 regular muffin cups by spraying with cooking spray.

2. Mix dry ingredients, including cheddar and chives, in a bowl. Add in buttermilk, butter, cream cheese, and 1 egg, and knead with your hands until completely combined.

3. Divide among muffin tins, gently pressing into the tins.

4. Beat remaining egg with water and brush tops of muffins with the mixture.

5. Bake for 25 minutes until a cake tester comes out clean.

Cheese and chives makes these individual soda breads interesting. These are great with just a salad or as an accompaniment to grilled fish.

CALORIES	170 calories
FAT	7.7 grams
PROTEIN	6.8 grams
SODIUM	248 mg
CARBOHYDRATES	17.3 grams
SUGARS	1.6 grams
FIBER	0.9 gram

mini chocolate zucchini muffins

Makes 24

1½ cups flour
½ cup sugar
1 egg
2 teaspoons baking powder
½ teaspoon salt
¼ cup vegetable oil
1 cup grated zucchini
2 tablespoons dark cocoa
   powder
½ cup skim milk
Optional: powdered sugar, for
   topping

1. Preheat oven to 400°F and prepare 24 mini muffin cups by spraying with cooking spray.

2. Mix all ingredients together well and divide among muffin cups, filling to the top.

3. Bake for 10 minutes until a cake tester comes out clean. Dust with powdered sugar if desired.

Shh. No one has to know that these muffins are packed with healthy zucchini. The fact that they're made in mini muffin size reinforces the idea that they are a treat!

CALORIES	73 calories
FAT	2.6 grams
PROTEIN	1.4 grams
SODIUM	46 mg
CARBOHYDRATES	10.9 grams
SUGARS	4.6 grams
FIBER	0.4 gram

irish brown bread squares

Makes 9–10

1 cup whole wheat flour
½ cup flour
¼ cup rolled oats
¼ cup oat bran
1 teaspoon brown sugar
½ teaspoon salt
½ teaspoon baking powder
½ teaspoon baking soda
¾ cup buttermilk
Butter, for serving

1. Preheat oven to 400°F and prepare 9 regular cups by spraying with cooking spray.

2. Mix dry ingredients, then stir in buttermilk.

3. Divide among cups.

4. Bake for 8 minutes until a cake tester comes out clean. Serve with butter.

This is a fun recipe to make in the new square muffin cups, because each person gets a tiny loaf of bread of their own. If you try it that way, it will make 6 squares and will take about 10 minutes to bake. If you are out of buttermilk, use milk with ¾ tablespoon lemon juice mixed in.

CALORIES	107 calories (based on 9 muffin yield)
FAT	1.2 grams
PROTEIN	4.5 grams
SODIUM	244 mg
CARBOHYDRATES	21.1 grams
SUGARS	1.7 grams
FIBER	2.5 grams

tea muffins with flavored butter

Makes 9

 Regular

½ cup skim milk
3 tea bags
1½ cups flour
½ cup sugar
2 teaspoons baking powder
½ teaspoon salt
1 egg
¼ cup vegetable oil
¼ teaspoon lemon extract

Flavored Butter
2 tablespoons unsalted butter, softened
1 tablespoon honey or jam

1. Preheat oven to 400°F and prepare 9 regular muffin cups by spraying with cooking spray.

2. Place milk in glass measuring cup and empty contents of tea bags into it (discard the bags once you empty them). Heat in the microwave until it boils. Allow to steep and cool.

3. Place flour, sugar, baking powder, and salt in a bowl and mix.

4. Add egg, vegetable oil, lemon extract, and tea/milk mixture and completely combine. Divide into muffin cups.

5. Bake for about 13 minutes until a cake tester comes out clean.

Flavored Butter

1. Process butter and honey or jam in food processor until mixed. Serve with muffins.

Try this recipe with different flavors of tea, for different tastes. The specks of tea leaves give this a fun appearance.

CALORIES	185 calories
FAT	6.7 grams
PROTEIN	3.2 grams
SODIUM	252 mg
CARBOHYDRATES	28 grams
SUGARS	11.9 grams
FIBER	0.5 gram

apple cinnamon scones with glaze or clotted cream

Makes 18

 Regular

3 cups flour

½ cup sugar

4 teaspoons baking powder

1 teaspoon salt

1½ sticks unsalted butter, cut into small pieces

1 cup heavy cream

¼ cup apple cider

2 apples, peeled, cored, and grated

2 teaspoons cinnamon

1½ tablespoons decorative sugar crystals

Optional: glaze for topping (see Kiwi Muffins with Glaze, earlier in this chapter)

Optional: clotted cream (see below for recipe)

Clotted Cream

1 cup heavy cream

1 cup sour cream

¼ cup powdered sugar

1. Preheat oven to 375°F and prepare 18 regular muffin cups by spraying with cooking spray.

2. Place flour, sugar, baking powder, salt, and butter in a bowl and use a pastry cutter to mix, or blend in a food processor until it resembles coarse meal.

3. Stir in cream, cider, apples, and cinnamon.

4. Divide among muffin cups, filling about ¾ full.

5. Sprinkle the tops with the sugar crystals.

6. Bake for about 30 minutes until a cake tester comes out clean. Drizzle with glaze or clotted cream.

Clotted Cream

1. Beat cream until whipped, then stir in sour cream and sugar.

This is a nontraditional take on scones, which are usually baked on a baking sheet and cut into triangles, or baked in a scone pan that is divided into triangles. If you have a cast iron muffin tin, try making this recipe in that, which will more closely replicate a scone pan. These scones freeze well, so you can make a lot and keep them frozen for breakfast in a flash. I love to serve scones with clotted cream and strawberry jam, as I enjoyed them in England. Don't forget a cup of tea to complete the snack!

CALORIES	244 calories (Scone only)	76 calories (Clotted Cream)
FAT	12 grams	6.7 grams
PROTEIN	2.4 grams	0.5 gram
SODIUM	249 mg	15 mg
CARBOHYDRATES	30.1 grams	2.4 grams
SUGARS	12.8 grams	2.1 grams
FIBER	0.7 gram	0 gram

ham and cheese muffins

Makes 9

 Regular

1½ cups flour
2 teaspoons baking powder
1 egg
½ cup skim milk
¼ cup vegetable oil
1 tablespoon Dijon mustard
½ cup shredded Swiss cheese
½ cup finely diced ham or
    chopped deli ham
⅛ teaspoon pepper

1. Preheat oven to 400°F and prepare 9 regular muffin cups by spraying with cooking spray.

2. Mix all ingredients in a bowl, then divide among muffin tins.

3. Bake for about 12 minutes or until a cake tester comes out clean.

This lunch-in-a-muffin is super portable and awfully cute. Cheddar cheese also works well in it.

CALORIES	175 calories
FAT	9 grams
PROTEIN	5.9 grams
SODIUM	238 mg
CARBOHYDRATES	17.6 grams
SUGARS	0.9 gram
FIBER	0.6 gram

mango coconut muffins

Makes 12

 Regular

1 cup flour
½ cup whole wheat pastry flour
¼ cup sugar
1 egg
2 teaspoons baking powder
½ teaspoon salt
1 cup canned mango, chopped
    with ¼ cup mango juice
    reserved
½ cup coconut milk
⅛ teaspoon nutmeg
¼ cup shredded coconut,
    toasted, plus 2 tablespoons
    for topping

1. Preheat oven to 400°F and prepare 12 regular muffin cups by spraying with cooking spray.

2. Place all ingredients in a bowl and mix until completely combined.

3. Divide among muffin cups and sprinkle reserved coconut on top.

4. Bake for about 12 minutes until a cake tester comes out clean.

Close your eyes and you could almost be on the beach in Hawaii when you enjoy these tropical muffins. You could add ¼ cup chopped macadamia nuts to this recipe to give some additional crunch, if you like. You can substitute fresh mango for canned, but you need to be sure to reserve juice from it (or buy it separately).

CALORIES	120 calories
FAT	3.3 grams
PROTEIN	2.4 grams
SODIUM	193 mg
CARBOHYDRATES	20.4 grams
SUGARS	7.7 grams
FIBER	1.3 grams

maple bacon muffins

Makes 10

 Regular

3 slices of bacon
1 cup flour
½ cup cornmeal
¼ cup sugar
2 teaspoons baking powder
½ teaspoon salt
½ cup buttermilk
1 egg
3 tablespoons maple syrup

1. Preheat oven to 400°F and prepare 10 regular muffin cups by spraying with cooking spray.

2. Cook bacon and reserve 1 tablespoon grease.

3. Mix flour, cornmeal, sugar, baking powder, and salt.

4. Mix buttermilk, egg, and bacon grease and add to dry ingredients.

5. Crumble bacon and stir in.

6. Stir in maple syrup.

7. Divide among muffin cups.

8. Bake for 8–10 minutes until a cake tester comes out clean.

These muffins are great for breakfast, but also work for lunch or dinner. The cornmeal gives them a little unexpected crunch.

CALORIES	129 calories
FAT	1.9 grams
PROTEIN	3.7 grams
SODIUM	289 mg
CARBOHYDRATES	24.2 grams
SUGARS	9.4 grams
FIBER	0.8 gram

buckwheat pear muffins with glaze

Makes 12

1 egg
½ cup plus 2 tablespoons skim
   milk
¼ cup vegetable oil
½ cup sugar
2 teaspoons baking powder
½ teaspoon salt
1 cup buckwheat flour
½ cup flour
1 pear, peeled, cored and
   chopped (about 1 cup)
¼ teaspoon nutmeg
¼ teaspoon cinnamon
Optional: glaze for topping (see
   Kiwi Muffins with Glaze, earlier in this chapter)

1. Preheat oven to 400°F, and prepare 12 regular muffin cups by spraying with cooking spray.

2. Mix egg, milk, oil and sugar, then add dry ingredients.

3. Stir in pear and spices.

4. Divide among muffin cups and bake for about 16 minutes. Drizzle with glaze if desired.

If you like buckwheat pancakes, you'll love these muffins. Use any variety of pear you have available.

CALORIES	157 calories
FAT	5.2 grams
PROTEIN	2.8 grams
SODIUM	192 mg
CARBOHYDRATES	22.3 grams
SUGARS	10.6 grams
FIBER	1.5 grams

pistachio orange chocolate chip muffins

Makes 10

 Regular

½ cup sugar
½ cup skim milk
¼ cup vegetable oil
1 egg
½ cup flour
1 cup whole wheat pastry flour
2 teaspoons baking powder
½ teaspoon salt
⅔ cup chopped unsalted
   pistachios, plus additional
   unchopped for topping
⅓ cup mini chocolate chips, plus
   additional for topping
1 teaspoon orange extract
1 tablespoon orange zest

1. Preheat oven to 400°F and prepare 10 regular muffin cups by spraying with cooking spray.

2. Mix sugar, milk, oil and egg, and add flour, baking powder and salt.

3. Stir in nuts, chocolate chips, orange extract, and zest.

4. Divide among muffin cups and place 3–4 whole unshelled pistachios on top of each, as well as ¼ teaspoon chocolate chips.

5. Bake for about 13 minutes until a cake tester comes out clean.

The unexpected combination of pistachios, orange, and chocolate chips, makes these muffins winners.

CALORIES	243 calories
FAT	11.2 grams
PROTEIN	4.5 grams
SODIUM	220 mg
CARBOHYDRATES	31.7 grams
SUGARS	15.6 grams
FIBER	2.2 grams

pumpkin maple walnut muffins with glaze

Makes 16

 Regular

¾ cup chopped walnuts, plus about 16 walnut halves
3 tablespoons maple syrup
1½ cups sugar
1 cup canned pumpkin (not pumpkin pie filling)
½ cup water
½ cup vegetable oil
2 eggs
1 cup flour
½ cup plus 2 tablespoons whole wheat pastry flour
½ teaspoon salt
½ teaspoon baking soda
2 teaspoons baking powder
1 teaspoon cinnamon
¼ teaspoon cloves
¼ teaspoon nutmeg
Optional: glaze for topping (from Kiwi Muffins with Glaze, earlier in this chapter)

1. Preheat oven to 400°F. Mix walnuts and maple syrup on a baking sheet that's been sprayed with cooking spray, spreading them out evenly and keeping the whole walnuts to one side.

2. Bake about 8–10 minutes, stirring frequently, until nuts are toasted and browned and syrup has hardened on them. Allow to cool.

3. Mix sugar, pumpkin, water, oil and eggs with a mixer.

4. Mix in both flours, salt, baking soda, baking powder, cinnamon, cloves, and nutmeg.

5. Stir in walnut pieces, reserving the halves.

6. Prepare 16 regular muffin cups by spraying with cooking spray.

7. Divide batter among muffin cups.

8. Divide walnut halves among the tops of the muffins and bake for about 15 minutes until a cake tester comes out clean. Drizzle with glaze, if desired.

This will quickly become one of your standard fall dishes once you taste the deep rich flavor and experience the moistness of these muffins.

CALORIES	240 calories
FAT	10.9 grams
PROTEIN	3 grams
SODIUM	183 mg
CARBOHYDRATES	33 grams
SUGARS	21.7 grams
FIBER	1.6 grams

Chapter 9

Desserts

Muffin tins are, of course, perfect for making cupcakes, but they also can make mini pies and mini versions of many of your other favorite treats. Think of them as a vehicle to create individual dishes, and you'll see that the choices are endless.

mini ice-cream cakes

Makes 6

 Regular

6 chocolate wafers
1 cup vanilla frozen yogurt or
  ice cream
6 vanilla wafers
1 cup chocolate frozen yogurt or
  ice cream
1 tablespoon rainbow sprinkles

1. Place 6 foil or silicone muffin cup liners in a regular muffin tin.

2. Place a chocolate wafer at the bottom of each.

3. Soften the vanilla frozen yogurt or ice cream, and spread on top of the wafer, smoothing it out.

4. Place in the freezer for 30 minutes.

5. Place a vanilla wafer in each cup.

6. Soften the chocolate frozen yogurt or ice cream, and spread that on top, smoothing it out.

7. Top with sprinkles.

8. Freeze for at least 1 hour, until hardened.

This fun dessert is incredibly versatile. You can use any flavors of frozen yogurt or ice cream you like. If you prefer two layers of chocolate wafers, do that. You can top this with whipped cream or a dab of chocolate sauce instead of sprinkles.

CALORIES	128 calories
FAT	4.1 grams
PROTEIN	2.5 grams
SODIUM	98 mg
CARBOHYDRATES	20.7 grams
SUGARS	13.1 grams
FIBER	1 gram

nectarine crisp with crumb topping

Makes 12

 Regular

4 nectarines, peeled and cut into thin slices

Crumb Topping
1 stick unsalted butter
1 cup whole wheat pastry flour
1 cup brown sugar
⅛ teaspoon salt
1 teaspoon cinnamon

1. Preheat oven to 350°F.

2. Place 12 foil or silicone liners in a regular muffin tin.

3. Divide fruit among the cups.

Crumb Topping

1. Pulse remaining ingredients in a food processor until they resemble coarse meal.

2. Fill the cups with the topping. You may not need all of it, and can freeze remaining topping for use at another time.

3. Bake for 15 minutes, until lightly browned on top and nectarines are soft.

Use this basic crisp recipe for any fall fruit, such as peaches, apples, or pears.

CALORIES	108 calories
FAT	3.7 grams
PROTEIN	1.1 grams
SODIUM	15 mg
CARBOHYDRATES	17.8 grams
SUGARS	12.6 grams
FIBER	1.4 grams

black-bottom strawberry cheesecake

Makes 12

 Regular

12 chocolate wafers
8 ounces light cream cheese
1 cup sugar
2 eggs
½ cup light sour cream
½ teaspoon vanilla
1 teaspoon orange zest
¼ cup flour
Pinch of salt

Topping
½ cup light sour cream
4 tablespoons strawberry jam
6 large strawberries, cleaned,
    hulled, and sliced

1. Preheat oven to 325°F.

2. Prepare 12 regular muffin cups with foil or silicone liners.

3. Place 1 wafer in the bottom of each cup.

4. Beat the cream cheese and sugar in a bowl on medium until smooth.

5. Beat in eggs on medium until combined.

6. Beat in sour cream, vanilla, and zest on medium until combined.

7. On low, beat in flour and salt until combined.

8. Divide the mixture among the cups.

9. Bake for 35 minutes until cheesecake is set.

10. Make topping: Stir sour cream and 2 tablespoons of jam together in a small bowl. Spread on top of the cheesecakes and return to the oven for 5 more minutes. Remove from oven and allow to cool.

11. Melt the remaining 2 tablespoons jam in the microwave.

12. Fan the strawberry slices out on top of the cheesecakes and brush with the melted jam.

You can use blueberry jam and blueberries instead of the strawberry jam and strawberries for a different flavor, or try using a gingersnap in place of the chocolate wafer.

CALORIES	197 calories
FAT	6.1 grams
PROTEIN	3.9 grams
SODIUM	169 mg
CARBOHYDRATES	31.1 grams
SUGARS	23.2 grams
FIBER	0.5 gram

peaches and cream mini pies

Makes 6

 Regular

1 refrigerated pie crust
4 peaches, peeled, pitted, and thinly sliced
2 tablespoons sugar
⅛ teaspoon nutmeg
1 tablespoon flour
1 tablespoon plus 1 teaspoon heavy cream
6 tablespoons Crumb Topping (see Nectarine Crisp with Crumb Topping, earlier in this chapter)

1. Preheat the oven to 350°F and prepare 6 regular muffin cups.

2. Follow instructions in "Using Pie Crusts" in the Introduction to prepare pie crusts. Place in cups.

3. Mix peaches and other ingredients in a bowl, then divide among the cups.

4. Top each with 1 tablespoon crumb topping.

5. Bake for about 27 minutes, until browned and bubbling. Allow to cool before removing from cups.

Better than your average peach pie, the addition of cream takes this pie to a whole new level.

CALORIES	243 calories
FAT	10.8 grams
PROTEIN	2 grams
SODIUM	166 mg
CARBOHYDRATES	36.8 grams
SUGARS	17.9 grams
FIBER	1.9 grams

chocolate chip cookie cups

Makes 18

 Regular

2 sticks unsalted butter
1 cup dark brown sugar
½ cup sugar
2 eggs
1 teaspoon vanilla
1¼ cups whole wheat pastry flour
1 cup flour
1 teaspoon salt
1 teaspoon baking soda
1½ cups chocolate chips
1 cup chopped nuts (optional)

1. Preheat the oven to 350°F, and prepare 18 regular muffin cups by spraying them with cooking spray.

2. Cream unsalted butter and sugar in a large bowl.

3. Beat in eggs and vanilla.

4. Beat in flours, salt, and baking soda.

5. Fold in chocolate chips and nuts (if using).

6. Using a cooking dough scoop, drop 2 scoops plus about a teaspoon of dough into each cup.

7. Using your fingers or a small spoon, press the dough around inside the cups, so that it comes up to the top edges in the shape of the cup.

8. Bake 20–25 minutes, until the cups are lightly browned. Note that as you bake them they will puff up, filling the entire cup, but by the time they are done, they will deflate.

9. Allow to cool completely.

10. Use a knife to loosen the cookie cups, then remove.

These cookie cups are very versatile. Fill them with a filling of your choice, such as frosting and sprinkles, pudding, mousse, whipped cream, or fresh sliced fruit.

CALORIES	361 calories (includes nuts)
FAT	19.3 grams
PROTEIN	5 grams
SODIUM	262 mg
CARBOHYDRATES	42.6 grams
SUGARS	28.5 grams
FIBER	1.7 grams

gram's chocolate cupcakes with easy buttercream frosting

Makes 18

 Mini

½ cup cocoa powder
1 cup Miracle Whip Light
1 cup sugar
1 teaspoon vanilla
2 cups flour
½ teaspoon salt
2 teaspoons baking soda dissolved in 1 cup boiling water

Easy Buttercream Frosting

1 stick unsalted butter
2 cups powdered sugar
½ teaspoon vanilla
1 tablespoon heavy cream

1. Preheat oven to 350°F and prepare 18 mini muffin cups by lining with paper liners.

2. Mix all ingredients together completely and divide among the cups using a cookie dough scoop.

3. Bake for about 18 minutes.

Easy Buttercream Frosting

1. Place all ingredients in a food processor and process until completely mixed. If you want chocolate frosting, add ¼ cup cocoa powder.

This was my grandmother's special chocolate cake recipe, which I've made into cupcakes. Note that there is no oil or eggs because the Miracle Whip provides all the moisture.

CALORIES	232 calories
FAT	5.9 grams
PROTEIN	2 grams
SODIUM	323 mg
CARBOHYDRATES	38.5 grams
SUGARS	25.7 grams
FIBER	1.1 grams

dirty blonde brownies

Makes 18

 Regular

⅔ cup unsalted butter, melted
2 cups brown sugar
2 eggs
2 teaspoons vanilla
1 cup flour
1 cup whole wheat pastry flour
1 teaspoon salt
1 teaspoon baking powder
½ cup mini chocolate chips
½ cup chopped nuts (optional)

1. Preheat oven to 350°F and prepare 18 regular muffin cups by spraying with cooking spray.

2. Mix unsalted butter and sugar.

3. Add eggs and vanilla.

4. Add flours, salt, and baking powder, and mix.

5. Stir in chocolate chips and nuts, if using.

6. Divide among muffin cups and bake for 30 minutes, until a cake tester comes out clean.

These brownies could be made with M&M's or Reese's Pieces. This is particularly fun if you choose seasonal or holiday colors.

CALORIES	266 calories (includes nuts)
FAT	10.7 grams
PROTEIN	3.2 grams
SODIUM	197 mg
CARBOHYDRATES	39.3 grams
SUGARS	27.6 grams
FIBER	1.2 grams

strawberry trifle

Makes 6

 Jumbo

4 slices pound cake
16 ounces prepared vanilla
   pudding
6 teaspoons strawberry jam
11 strawberries, hulled and
   sliced

1. Prepare 6 jumbo muffin cups with foil or silicone liners.

2. Cut 2 of the pound cake slices into cubes (about ½"), and divide among the bottoms of the cups, pressing slightly into the cup.

3. Top with ½ the vanilla pudding, divided among the cups.

4. Place ½ teaspoon strawberry jam on top of the pudding, and spread it around.

5. Top with half the strawberries.

6. Cube the rest of the pound cake and divide among cups, pressing down.

7. Top with the rest of the pudding, divided.

8. Add the rest of the strawberries, fanning the slices out, then brush them with the remaining jam.

9. Refrigerate at least 3 hours, up to 8.

This dessert is fun to serve for the 4th of July, particularly if you add a few blueberries to the top of the cups. You can make this in jumbo jumbo individual silicone muffin cups, for easy serving as well.

CALORIES	266 calories
FAT	8.8 grams
PROTEIN	3.7 grams
SODIUM	252 mg
CARBOHYDRATES	42.2 grams
SUGARS	23.8 grams
FIBER	1.1 grams

trashed krispies

Makes 18

 Regular

2 cups Rice Chex cereal
1½ cups Rice Krispies cereal
1½ cups mini pretzels
1 cup party peanuts
¼ cup unsalted butter
10 ounces marshmallows, regular size (1 package)
¼ cup semisweet chocolate chips

1. Prepare 18 regular muffin cups by spraying with cooking spray.

2. Mix dry ingredients in a bowl.

3. Melt butter in a large saucepan.

4. Stir in marshmallows and chocolate chips until dissolved.

5. Stir in dry ingredients.

6. Using a greased squeezable ice cream scoop, place one scoop in each muffin cup.

7. Spray your hands with cooking spray and press down on the treats.

8. Allow to rest and set up before serving.

You can use any dry cereal you like in this recipe. Just be sure you have 6 cups total of dry ingredients, including the nuts.

CALORIES	144 calories
FAT	5.1 grams
PROTEIN	2.6 grams
SODIUM	125 mg
CARBOHYDRATES	23 grams
SUGARS	11.7 grams
FIBER	0.6 gram

caramel apple mini pies

Makes 6

 Regular

1 unbaked refrigerated pie crust
2 apples, peeled, cored, and
   thinly sliced, then cut in half
   so they are shorter
Pinch of salt
2 teaspoons flour
2 teaspoons sugar
¼ teaspoon cinnamon
2 tablespoons caramel sauce
1 egg
1 teaspoon water

1. Preheat oven to 350°F and prepare 6 regular muffin cups.

2. Follow the instructions in "Using Pie Crusts" in the Introduction to prepare the pie crust. Place in cups. Keep the scraps.

3. Mix apples, salt, flour, sugar, cinnamon, and caramel sauce in a bowl.

4. Divide filling among muffin cups.

5. Use ½–1" scraps of pie crust and dot the tops of the pies with them.

6. Cover with foil and bake for 30 minutes. Remove from oven.

7. Mix egg with 1 teaspoon water and brush tops of pies.

8. Return to oven uncovered for 20 minutes, until apples are tender and crust is golden.

Apple pie becomes decadent with the addition of caramel sauce in these mini pies.

CALORIES	183 calories
FAT	8 grams
PROTEIN	2 grams
SODIUM	215 mg
CARBOHYDRATES	27.9 grams
SUGARS	6.9 grams
FIBER	0.8 gram

molasses bites

Makes 36

 Mini

¾ cup unsalted butter, softened
1 cup brown sugar
1 egg
¼ cup blackstrap molasses
1¼ cups flour
1 cup whole wheat pastry flour
¼ teaspoon salt
1 teaspoon cinnamon
1 teaspoon ground ginger
Sanding sugar

1. Preheat oven to 375°F and prepare 36 mini muffin cups by spraying with cooking spray.

2. Mix butter and sugar, then add egg and molasses and beat until blended.

3. Add flours, salt, cinnamon and ginger and mix until completely blended.

4. Using a cookie dough scoop, divide among the muffin cups.

5. Lightly brush the tops of the cookies with water, then sprinkle on a pinch of sanding sugar on each.

6. Bake for 14 minutes until bites spring back to the touch.

Make this when you need to take cookies somewhere but don't feel like worrying about spacing them on baking sheets and making them perfectly round. The muffin tins do the work for you.

CALORIES	84 calories
FAT	3.8 grams
PROTEIN	0.7 gram
SODIUM	21 mg
CARBOHYDRATES	11.8 grams
SUGARS	8.1 grams
FIBER	0.4 gram

pumpkin ginger mini pies

Makes 18

 Regular

1 15-ounce can pumpkin (not pumpkin pie mix)
1 12-ounce can evaporated fat-free milk
¾ cup sugar
2 eggs
½ teaspoon salt
2 teaspoons pumpkin pie spice
18 gingersnap cookies

1. Preheat oven to 350°F and prepare 18 regular muffin cups with foil or silicone liners.

2. Mix pumpkin, milk, sugar, eggs, salt, and spice with a mixer until blended.

3. Place 1 gingersnap in each muffin cup.

4. Divide pumpkin mixture among the cups, filling about ¾ full. The pumpkin mixture will be absorbed into the cookie and you'll need to go back and add more filling to each cup.

5. The ginger snaps should float to the top. If any do not, simply nudge them with a fork and they will float up (and if they don't, depending on the density of the brand you use, that's okay, let them be the bottom crust instead of the top).

6. Bake for 30 minutes until pumpkin is set. Serve with whipped cream.

Gingersnaps add an unexpected kick of flavor to pumpkin mini pies in this recipe.

CALORIES	97 calories
FAT	1.2 grams
PROTEIN	2.8 grams
SODIUM	127 mg
CARBOHYDRATES	18.7 grams
SUGARS	14.2 grams
FIBER	0.8 gram

butter pecan cupcakes with frosting

Makes 20

Regular

1⅓ cup chopped pecans
1 tablespoon unsalted butter, melted
⅔ cup unsalted butter
1⅓ cup sugar
2 eggs
2 cups flour
1½ teaspoons baking powder
¼ teaspoon salt
1½ teaspoons vanilla
⅓ cup light sour cream
⅓ cup skim milk

Frosting
3 tablespoons unsalted butter
2 tablespoons brown sugar
3 cups powdered sugar
3 tablespoons skim milk
1 tablespoon heavy cream

1. Preheat oven to 350°F and prepare 20 regular cupcake tins with paper liners.

2. Place pecans on a baking sheet. Drizzle with the melted butter. Toast, tossing occasionally, about 5–7 minutes, until lightly browned.

3. Cream butter and sugar in a large bowl. Beat in eggs.

4. Add half the flour and all of the baking powder, salt, and vanilla and beat.

5. Add sour cream and beat.

6. Add remaining 1 cup flour and beat.

7. Add milk and beat.

8. Stir in 1 cup of the nuts. Divide among cupcake tins, filling each ¾ full.

9. Bake for about 20 minutes until a cake tester comes out clean. Allow cupcakes to cool.

Frosting

1. Melt butter and brown sugar in a bowl in the microwave, stirring occasionally until the sugar is dissolved.

2. Pour into a food processor and add powdered sugar, milk, and cream.

3. Pulse until combined and smooth.

4. Add remaining ⅓ cup nuts and pulse to combine completely.

5. Spread frosting on cooled cupcakes.

CALORIES	313 calories
FAT	14 grams
PROTEIN	3 grams
SODIUM	81 mg
CARBOHYDRATES	43.6 grams
SUGARS	32.7 grams
FIBER	1 gram

I took these cupcakes to my husband's office, and they vanished in minutes. Sour cream adds richness and moisture to the batter, and the frosting takes them to new heights.

croissant bread pudding

Makes 4

 Jumbo

3 croissants, torn into 1" pieces
1 egg
½ cup heavy cream
¼ cup mini chocolate chips
⅛ teaspoon nutmeg
⅛ teaspoon cinnamon
1 tablespoon sugar

1. Preheat oven to 350°F and prepare 4 jumbo muffin cups with foil or silicone liners.

2. Mix all ingredients together.

3. Divide among muffin cups.

4. Bake for 20 minutes until the dessert is set and golden on top.

CALORIES	325 calories
FAT	21.3 grams
PROTEIN	5.8 grams
SODIUM	138 mg
CARBOHYDRATES	27.5 grams
SUGARS	14.7 grams
FIBER	0.8 gram

There's something so comforting about bread pudding, and when you make it with croissants, it becomes even richer. Melt a little strawberry jelly in the microwave oven to drizzle on top of these for some extra color and flavor.

date and nut bites

Makes 24

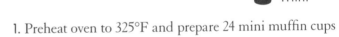 Mini

2 eggs
½ cup sugar
½ teaspoon vanilla
½ cup flour
½ teaspoon baking powder
¼ teaspoon salt
1 cup chopped walnuts
2 cups chopped dates

1. Preheat oven to 325°F and prepare 24 mini muffin cups with paper, foil, or silicone liners.

2. Beat eggs until foamy, then beat in sugar and vanilla.

3. Mix in flour, baking powder, and salt, then stir in walnuts and dates.

4. Divide among muffin tins and bake for 25 minutes until a cake tester comes out clean.

CALORIES	102 calories
FAT	3.4 grams
PROTEIN	1.8 grams
SODIUM	40 mg
CARBOHYDRATES	16.1 grams
SUGARS	12.1 grams
FIBER	1.4 grams

Feel virtuous when you make these bites because they are packed with dates and nuts. No one will think of that when you serve it though, and will just focus on the rich flavor and deep moistness.

blueberry mini pies

Makes 6

 Regular

1 premade unbaked refrigerated
    pie crust
2 cups fresh blueberries, divided
    (frozen works well also)
⅓ cup sugar
⅓ cup water
2 tablespoons cornstarch
½ teaspoon lemon juice
Pinch salt
Pinch cinnamon
Whipped cream, for serving

1. Preheat oven to 350°F and prepare 6 regular muffin cups.

2. Cut 6 circles out of the pie crust using the method described in "Using Pie Crust" in the Introduction.

3. Place the pie crust circles in the muffin tins, pushing down into the cup.

4. Place 1 cup of the blueberries, the sugar, water, cornstarch, lemon juice, salt, and cinnamon in a medium saucepan and heat until boiling. Then cook about 2 minutes until thickened.

5. Stir in remaining 1 cup blueberries and divide mixture among muffin cups.

6. Bake about 20 minutes until pies are set and crust is golden. Serve with whipped cream.

You can add the Crumb Topping (see Nectarine Crisp with Crumb Topping, earlier in this chapter) to the top of these pies before baking, if you like a topping on your pie.

CALORIES	210 calories
FAT	7.3 grams
PROTEIN	1 gram
SODIUM	180 mg
CARBOHYDRATES	35.1 grams
SUGARS	16 grams
FIBER	1.2 grams

mini fondue

Makes 4

 Regular

¼ cup heavy cream
½ cup semisweet chocolate chips
For dipping: bite-size pieces of pound cake, strawberries, blueberries, bananas, pineapple, marshmallow, or crispy rice treats

1. Preheat oven to 350°F and prepare 4 regular muffin cups by lining with silicone cups.

2. Place 1 teaspoon cream in the bottom of each cup.

3. Top with 2 tablespoons chocolate chips.

4. Top with 2 teaspoons cream.

5. Bake for 8–10 minutes, removing from the oven every 3–4 minutes to stir each cup to combine.

6. Serve with bite-size dipping morsels.

This is a great way to make fondue that is portion controlled with no risk of double dipping. It's also perfect for children, because they don't have to try to reach the big, hot fondue pot. Use high-quality chocolate for the best results. For a variation, replace half the chocolate chips with peanut butter chips. Note that these take a bit longer to melt, so you will need to increase your baking time about 5 minutes.

CALORIES	91 calories (Fondue only)
FAT	7.2 grams
PROTEIN	0.8 gram
SODIUM	10 mg
CARBOHYDRATES	5.4 grams
SUGARS	4.5 grams
FIBER	0.5 gram

poppy seed cupcakes

Makes 24

 Regular

1 1.25-ounce container of poppy
    seeds
¾ cup skim milk
⅔ cup softened unsalted butter
1½ cups sugar
¼ cup heavy cream
1 teaspoon vanilla
2 cups cake flour
2½ teaspoons baking powder
½ teaspoon salt
4 egg whites
7 tablespoons strawberry jam
7 tablespoons whipped cream,
    or to taste

1. Soak poppy seeds in milk for 1–2 hours.

2. Preheat oven to 350°F and prepare 24 regular muffin cups with paper liners.

3. Cream unsalted butter and sugar. Set aside.

4. Add cream and vanilla to poppy seed mixture.

5. In another bowl, mix cake flour, baking powder and salt.

6. Alternate adding the dry ingredients and the milk mixture into the creamed butter mixture, beating until combined.

7. In a separate bowl, beat egg whites until they have stiff peaks, then fold into the cake batter.

8. Divide batter among the muffin tins, filling about ¾ full.

9. Bake for 17–20 minutes until just barely done, by testing with a cake tester, then allow to cool. Be careful not to overbake this: it tastes best when the cake is very moist and almost underdone.

10. Top each cupcake with about a teaspoon of strawberry jam spread on top, then a dollop of whipped cream. Serve immediately.

I love the soft texture of these white cupcakes, heavily dotted with pretty poppy seeds.

CALORIES	175 calories
FAT	6.5 grams
PROTEIN	2.1 grams
SODIUM	116 mg
CARBOHYDRATES	26.5 grams
SUGARS	15.8 grams
FIBER	0.6 gram

shortbread brownies

Makes 9

 Regular

13⅓ tablespoons unsalted butter, divided
2 tablespoons brown sugar
1¼ cups flour, divided
2 ounces bittersweet chocolate
1 cup sugar
1½ teaspoons baking powder
½ teaspoon salt
1 teaspoon vanilla
1 egg

1. Preheat oven to 325°F and prepare 9 regular muffin cups by spraying with cooking spray or lining with silicone liners.

2. Mix 8 tablespoons butter, brown sugar, and ½ cup flour with a mixer, until combined.

3. Divide among muffin tins and bake for 7 minutes.

4. Place remaining 5⅓ tablespoons butter and chocolate in a bowl, and melt in microwave about 1–2 minutes until chocolate is just barely melted, stirring often. Allow to cool.

5. Place remaining ¾ cup flour, sugar, baking powder, and salt in a bowl, and mix.

6. Add chocolate, vanilla, and egg, and mix completely.

7. Divide among muffin tins, pouring on top of shortbread crust.

8. Increase oven temperature to 350°F, and bake for 25 minutes, until brownie is cooked through.

These brownies have a surprise. The bottom crust is made of shortbread, so you can enjoy two desserts in one here.

CALORIES	340 calories
FAT	20 grams
PROTEIN	3 grams
SODIUM	223 mg
CARBOHYDRATES	38 grams
SUGARS	25.4 grams
FIBER	1.4 grams

apple cupcakes

Makes 9

 Regular

½ cup vegetable oil
¾ cup sugar
1 egg
1 cup flour
½ teaspoon baking powder
1 teaspoon cinnamon
Pinch of nutmeg
Pinch of salt
1 cup grated apple (core and
    skin removed), about 1 large
    apple
⅓ cup chopped pecans
½ teaspoon vanilla
Frosting: ½ batch of the frosting
    in Butter Pecan Cupcakes with
    Frosting, earlier in this chapter

1. Preheat oven to 350°F and prepare 9 regular muffin cups with silicone, paper, or foil liners.

2. Mix oil and sugar, then stir in egg.

3. Add flour, baking powder, cinnamon, nutmeg, and salt. Stir in apple, pecans, and vanilla.

4. Divide among cups, and bake for 22–25 minutes, until a cake tester comes out clean. Cupcakes will be very moist.

5. Make frosting and frost cupcakes with it.

These cupcakes are moister than anything you've ever tried. They are a perfect fall dessert. Use any variety of apple you like.

CALORIES	383 calories (including frosting)
FAT	18 grams
PROTEIN	2.7 grams
SODIUM	54 mg
CARBOHYDRATES	52.7 grams
SUGARS	40.5 grams
FIBER	1 gram

pineapple upside-down cakes

Makes 12

 Regular

5 tablespoons unsalted butter, melted

⅓ cup brown sugar

12 maraschino cherries, without stems

1 20-ounce can pineapple chunks, juice reserved

1 cup flour

½ cup sugar

½ teaspoon baking powder

¼ cup softened unsalted butter

1 egg

¼ teaspoon salt

½ cup pineapple juice, from can of pineapple chunks

½ teaspoon vanilla

1. Preheat oven to 350°F and prepare 12 nonstick muffin cups by spraying with cooking spray, or 12 silicone muffin cups by spraying with cooking spray.

2. Mix melted butter and brown sugar and divide among muffin tins.

3. Place 1 cherry in the center of each cup.

4. Drain the pineapple, reserving the juice. Pat the chunks dry with paper towels.

5. Place 3 or 4 chunks in the bottom of each cup, around the cherry (you may have to squeeze them in if your chunks are on the large side).

6. Mix remaining ingredients in a bowl. Divide among the muffin cups.

7. Bake for 25–30 minutes (cakes cooked directly in the muffin tin cook faster than those in a liner), testing for doneness with a cake tester.

8. Allow to cool for about 5 minutes, and invert to remove the cakes onto a plate or platter. You may need to run a knife around the side of each one to be sure it will pop out easily.

Silicone liners make these cute little desserts pop out completely intact and beautiful, but they also work in regular muffin cups. Just be sure to have the entire muffin pan covered when you flip it over.

CALORIES	229 calories
FAT	8.6 grams
PROTEIN	1.8 grams
SODIUM	29 mg
CARBOHYDRATES	36 grams
SUGARS	17.3 grams
FIBER	0.8 gram

lemon pudding cake

Makes 18

 Regular

2 eggs, separated
1 teaspoon lemon zest
⅔ cup skim milk
1 cup sugar
¼ cup flour
¼ teaspoon salt
¼ cup lemon juice

1. Preheat oven to 400°F.

2. Prepare 18 regular muffin cups with silicone liners.

3. Whisk egg yolks, zest, milk, sugar, flour, salt and lemon juice until combined.

4. In a separate bowl, beat egg whites until stiff peaks form.

5. Fold into batter until combined.

6. Fill muffin cups ¾ full.

7. Place muffin tin tray in a roasting pan filled with ½" hot water (you may need two roasting pans to fit all of your muffin tins).

8. Bake for 12 minutes until the top is lightly golden brown and pudding is set.

9. Allow to cool and serve in the cups.

This dessert is magic. You pour it into the cups as a very loose batter, and it bakes up with a cake on top and pudding on the bottom. They are cute served with a sprig of mint on top.

CALORIES	61 calories
FAT	0.5 gram
PROTEIN	1.2 grams
SODIUM	45 mg
CARBOHYDRATES	13.2 grams
SUGARS	11.7 grams
FIBER	0.1 gram

chocolate lava cakes

Makes 12

 Regular

2 sticks butter (1 cup)
2 ounces bittersweet baking
   chocolate
2 ounces dark chocolate
2 whole eggs
2 egg yolks
¼ cup sugar
2 teaspoons flour
Whipped cream or vanilla ice
   cream, for serving

1. Preheat oven to 450°F and prepare 12 silicone muffin liners by spraying with cooking spray.

2. Melt butter and chocolate in microwave, stirring frequently.

3. Whisk whole eggs, yolks, and sugar until light and thick. Whisk in flour.

4. Temper the egg mixture by adding in a little of the chocolate-and-butter mixture.

5. Whisk in the remaining chocolate-and-butter mixture.

6. Pour into the muffin cups.

7. Bake for 5–6 minutes, until the edges are set but the centers are very soft.

8. Allow to cool about 5 minutes, then remove the cups from the tin and upend them on plates to serve. Serve with whipped cream or vanilla ice cream.

Another magic dessert, these little cakes have a hidden molten chocolate center. Be careful not to overbake them.

CALORIES	224 calories
FAT	20 grams
PROTEIN	2.6 grams
SODIUM	16 mg
CARBOHYDRATES	8.5 grams
SUGARS	6 grams
FIBER	1.2 grams

lemon pound cake

Makes 9

 Regular

1 stick butter
¼ cup vegetable oil
1½ cups sugar
2 eggs
¼ teaspoon salt
½ teaspoon vanilla
½ cup light sour cream
1½ cups cake flour
½ teaspoon pure lemon extract
Zest of 1 lemon

1. Preheat oven to 350°F and prepare 9 regular muffin cups by spraying with cooking spray.

2. Mix butter, oil, and sugar in a bowl.

3. Beat in eggs, salt and vanilla.

4. Mix in sour cream, then cake flour.

5. Beat in lemon extract and zest, then divide batter among muffin cups.

6. Bake for about 13 minutes until a cake tester comes out clean.

I love serving individual pound cakes to guests with some fresh whipped cream and berries. You could add 1 tablespoon poppy seeds to this for a variation. If you make this in a square muffin tin, it will make 9 and will take about 19 minutes to bake.

CALORIES	390 calories
FAT	17.8 grams
PROTEIN	3.8 grams
SODIUM	91 mg
CARBOHYDRATES	52.2 grams
SUGARS	33.4 grams
FIBER	0.4 gram

crunchy peanut cupcakes

Makes 18

 Regular

1½ cups cake flour
½ cup sugar
2 teaspoons baking powder
½ teaspoon salt
1 cup crunchy peanut butter
½ cup brown sugar
1 egg
¼ cup vegetable oil
1 cup milk
¾ cup chocolate chips, divided
½ cup peanut butter chips,
    divided

1. Preheat oven to 400°F and prepare 18 regular muffin cups with paper liners (tulip liners work well for this recipe).

2. Mix flour, sugar, baking powder, salt, peanut butter, and brown sugar until crumbly. Reserve ½ cup of mixture.

3. Add egg, oil, and milk to the mixture, and combine completely.

4. Add ½ cup chocolate chips and ¼ cup peanut butter chips to mixture, then divide among muffin cups.

5. Mix reserved peanut butter mixture with ¼ cup chocolate chips and ¼ cup peanut chips, then sprinkle on top of cupcakes.

6. Bake for 20 minutes, then turn the heat down to 350°F and bake for another 8 minutes, until a cake tester comes out clean.

The crunchy topping makes these cupcakes very special.

CALORIES	257 calories
FAT	12.6 grams
PROTEIN	6.3 grams
SODIUM	220 mg
CARBOHYDRATES	29.6 grams
SUGARS	17.6 grams
FIBER	1.5 grams

cookies and cream cupcakes with oreo frosting

Makes 18

Regular

⅔ cup butter, softened
1 cup sugar
17 Double Stuf Oreos, divided
2 eggs
2 cups flour
1½ teaspoons baking powder
¼ teaspoon salt
1½ teaspoons vanilla
⅓ cup light sour cream
⅓ cup skim milk

Oreo Frosting

5 tablespoons butter, softened
14 chocolate wafers from Oreos,
    reserved from cupcake recipe
2 cups powdered sugar
3 tablespoons skim milk

1. Preheat oven to 350°F and line 18 regular muffin cups with paper, foil, or silicone liners.

2. Cream butter and sugar.

3. Take 7 Oreos and open them up. Scrape the filling out and add filling to the batter and mix well. Reserve the outsides of the cookies for frosting.

4. Beat in eggs.

5. Add flour, baking powder, salt, vanilla, sour cream, and milk and combine completely.

6. Take 6 whole Oreos and place them in a ziptop bag and completely crush them, then add to the batter (some small pieces will remain stuck to the inside of the bag; you don't need to scrape them out). Combine into the batter.

7. Take the remaining 4 whole Oreos and break into 4 or 5 pieces each. Stir into the batter.

8. Divide among muffin cups, and bake for 20–24 minutes, until a cake tester comes out clean. Allow to cool, then frost.

Oreo Frosting

1. Place all ingredients in a food processor and process to completely combine until smooth.

My testers went crazy for these cupcakes, which have a very intense Oreo flavor. You've got to have these with a tall glass of cold milk.

CALORIES	317 calories
FAT	13.7 grams
PROTEIN	2.6 grams
SODIUM	127 mg
CARBOHYDRATES	45.8 grams
SUGARS	30.8 grams
FIBER	0.3 gram

hot chocolate muffins

Makes 10

 Regular

½ cup skim milk
½ cup hot cocoa mix
1 teaspoon cocoa powder
1½ cups flour
¼ cup sugar
2 teaspoons baking powder
½ teaspoon salt
1 egg
¼ cup vegetable oil
¾ cup mini marshmallows,
  divided

1. Preheat oven to 400°F and prepare 10 regular muffin cups by spraying with cooking spray.

2. Place milk, cocoa mix, and cocoa powder in a glass measuring cup and heat in microwave until it just comes to a boil, about 1–2 minutes. Whisk until it is completely combined, then allow to cool.

3. Place flour, sugar, baking powder, and salt in a bowl.

4. Mix in milk-cocoa mixture, egg, and oil.

5. Stir in ½ cup mini marshmallows. Divide among muffin cups.

6. Divide remaining marshmallows among the cups, placing on the tops of the muffins.

7. Bake for about 13 minutes until a cake tester comes out clean.

Don't be surprised when you bite into one of these and there are no marshmallows inside! The heat of the baking process breaks them down and they get absorbed into the muffins, but still add flavor.

CALORIES	250 calories
FAT	7 grams
PROTEIN	4.5 grams
SODIUM	343 mg
CARBOHYDRATES	42.1 grams
SUGARS	22.6 grams
FIBER	1.3 grams

Acknowledgments

Thank you to my amazing agent, Gina Panettieri, for working faithfully and tirelessly on this project. To the terrific team at Adams Media, including Paula Munier, Jennifer Lawler, Frank Rivera, Matt Glazer, and Casey Ebert, thank you for your help and support in bringing my vision to fruition!

Fred Minnick, you were a joy to work with, and I am grateful to count you as a friend.

Many thanks to my writing friends, who are always, always there for me: Sheryl Kraft, Roxanne Hawn, Claudine Jalajas, Peggy Bourjaily, Kris Bordessa, Donna Hull, Ruth Pennebaker, Alisa Bowman, Christine Gross-Loh, Casey Barber, Kristin Gough, Meredith Resnick, Sarah Henry, Alexandra Grabbe, Debbie Koenig, Kerri Fivecoat-Campbell, Jane Boursaw, Jennifer Margulis, Jeanine Barone, Judy Stock, Melanie McMinn, Stephanie Auteri, Stephanie Stiavetti, Susan Johnston, Vera Marie Badertscher, Belle Wong, and Kerry Dexter. Your support means the world to me.

I need to take a minute to thank everyone who has visited, read, commented on, or just popped in at my blogs. Your interest and support are so important to me, and I appreciate the time you spend with me.

Thanks to everyone at Chakra Communications, Inc., who tested my recipes with enthusiasm and, apparently, extreme hunger bordering on starvation. Now you can have all the recipes for everything you loved!

Mom and Dad, thank you for everything. And to Gai and Gram, who are, I hope, watching over me in my kitchen endeavors, you are always with me.

With love and gratitude to my husband, Terry Sember, without whom this book could not have happened, and who makes everything possible. And to my own in-house muffin mouths, Quinne and Zayne, I love and adore you both. Dinner tonight will not be round.

About the Author

Brette Sember is the author of *The Parchment Paper Cookbook* (Adams Media) and *The Organized Kitchen* (Adams Media). She blogs about cooking at *www.MuffinTinFood.com*, *www.NoPotCooking.com*, and *www.MarthaAndMe.net*. Visit her website at *www.BretteSember.com*.